THE ISLANDS SERIES

Canary Islands: FUERTEVENTURA

THE ISLANDS SERIES

†The Aran Islands
The Isle of Arran
*Canary Islands: Fuerteventura
*Corsica
*The Falkland Islands
*Grand Bahama
†Harris and Lewis
Lundy
†The Isle of Mull
The Maltese Islands
†Orkney
St Kilda and the other Hebridean Outliers
*The Seychelles
†Shetland
*Singapore
*The Solomon Islands
*Vancouver Island

in preparation
Cyprus
Dominica
Puerto Rico
Skye
and many others

* Published in the United States by Stackpole
† Published in the United States by David & Charles

Canary Islands: FUERTEVENTURA

JOHN MERCER

DAVID & CHARLES : NEWTON ABBOT

STACKPOLE BOOKS : HARRISBURG

This edition first published in 1973
in Great Britain by David & Charles (Holdings) Limited
Newton Abbot Devon
in the United States by Stackpole Books
Harrisburg Pa.

ISBN 0 7153 5721 2 (*Great Britain*)

ISBN 0 8117 0031 1 (*United States*)

To

Francisco Brito

and

Salvador Santana

*Set in eleven on thirteen point Baskerville
and printed in Great Britain by
Clarke Doble & Brendon Limited Plymouth*

CONTENTS

ILLUSTRATIONS

6

ILLUSTRATIONS

MAPS

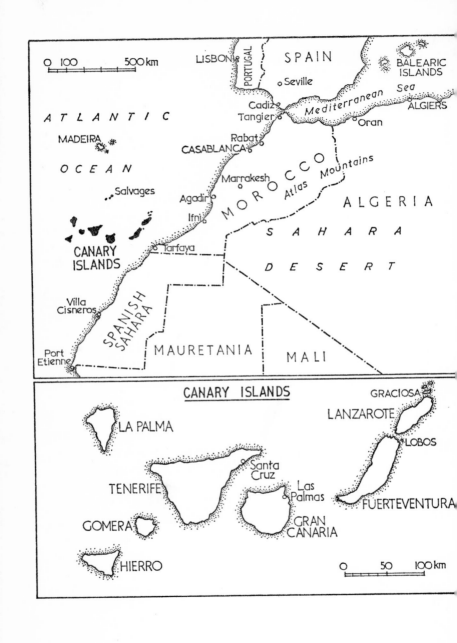

1   LANDSCAPE

IN 1534 there was published in Seville a 'New, amended and
enlarged history of the good gentleman Tristan of Lyonesse'.
At this time, about forty years after the defeat of the Moors
at Granada and three years before the birth of the author of
Don Quixote, the most popular books in Spain were stories of
chivalry. In translating one of the King Arthur legends into
Castilian, the Sevillian writer decided to give the story a Spanish
flavour. Reaching the point at which Tristan and Isolde land
upon an island and overcome an enchantment which includes
battling with two giants, the sixteenth-century author searched
his imagination for a background. Columbus had recently discovered the New World, Cortes had already destroyed the Aztecs,
and, even as he wrote, the Sevillian was hearing of Pizarro's
progress in his conquest of the Incas. Nevertheless, for sheer
fantasy, as a place where his audience would accept enchant-
ments and giants, he chose the island of Fuerteventura.

An island desert some fifty sea-miles off the north-west coast
of Africa, visible from the Sahara, Fuerteventura is one of the
easternmost Canaries. Seen from the deck of an approaching
steamer, the island appears to consist only of brown mountains
and brown plains, barren, dry, dusty, the coast steeply overhanging the sea. From the air, the nakedness of the landscape causes
the deeply-cut drainage patterns to dominate, with a black patch
of lava or a spread of yellow sand occasionally superimposed on
the brown desert. In the mind's eye Fuerteventura comes eventually to resemble a very old wrinkled brown-skinned crone,
long infertile and dried-up, quietly resigned, to be listened to
for the wisdom of her many experiences.

FUERTEVENTURA

Drought and goats are the everyday features of the island. Rainfall is often negligible for many years at a time, and the island's ground-water sources are clearly diminishing. In 1404, for example, the conquest chroniclers wrote of vigorously running streams, and thought that water-mills could be made in four or five places: a number of salt-saturated trickling rivulets are all that now remain, and even these are still dwindling. The islanders' ingenious irrigation schemes and spasmodic hard work cannot hope to compensate for the lowering of the water-table and the lack of rain. During the droughts the steadily increasing country population has always subsisted, as it does at present, upon the goats; and because of them, of course, the island stays utterly without vegetation; and this, in turn, accelerates evaporation and erosion, discourages condensation and rainfall. Within this constraining circle little can change, and in the country people there is alive the resigned, pessimistic spirit of all those who have undergone 'the years of hunger' before them. Nebulous early immigrants from north-west Africa who turn into the clearer conquest-people, the near-exterminated Mahohs, thoroughly mixed, in the fifteenth and sixteenth centuries, with Europeans, Moors and Negroes, all the inhabitants now have Spanish nationality. But the way of life has been modelled by the same local factors throughout: drought and goats.

Fuerteventura is about one hundred kms long; the width varies between twenty and thirty in the centre, drops to a mere five kms at the isthmus, then finally bulges to twice this on the south-western peninsula. About 1,700sq km in area, it is only a little smaller than Gran Canaria, the largest of the archipelago; but its population, about 18,000, of whom 5,000 live in the capital, Puerto del Rosario, is only five per cent that of Gran Canaria. The Spanish military map (1959 edition, 1:100,000) shows that, although the highest of Fuerteventura's peaks is a mere 807m above sea-level, there are a great many of them. One mountain chain, broken up by deep ravines, or *barrancos*, entirely covers the southern peninsula and, in fact, almost the whole of the southern third of the island, and then, in a broad

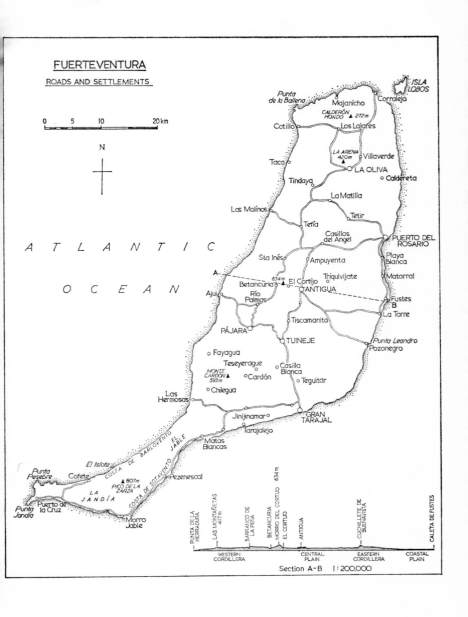

FUERTEVENTURA

ROADS AND SETTLEMENTS

0   5   10   20 km

N

ATLANTIC

OCEAN

ISLA LOBOS

Punta de la Ballena

Corralejo

Majanicho

CALDERÓN HONDO ▲ 272 m

Cotillo

Los Lajares

LA ARENA 420 m ▲

Villaverde

Taca

LA OLIVA

Caldereta

Tindaya

La Matilla

Las Molinos

Tetir

Tefía

Casillas del Angel

PUERTO DEL ROSARIO

Sta Inés

Ampuyenta

Playa Blanca

A

634 m

El Cortijo

Triquivijate

Matorral

Betancuria ▲

ANTIGUA

Fustes

Ajuí

Río Palmas

B

La Torre

Tiscamanita

PÁJARA

TUINEJE

Punta Leandro

Pozonegro

Fayagua

Teseyerague

MONTE CARDÓN ▲ 593 m

Cardón

Casilla Blanca

Chilegua

Teguitar

Las Hermosas

GRAN TARAJAL

Jinijinamar

Tarajalejo

Matas Blancas

EL JABLE

COSTA DE BARLOVENTO

El Islote

Pezenescal

Cofete

Punta Pesebre

▲ 807 m PICO DE LA ZARZA

COSTA DE SOTAVENTO

LA JANDÍA

Puerto de la Cruz

Punta Jandía

Morro Jable

PUNTA DE LA HERRADURA

LAS MONTAÑETAS 417 m

BARRANCO DE LA PEÑA

BETANCURIA

MORRO DEL CORTIJO 634 m

EL CORTIJO

ANTIGUA

CUCHILLETE DE BUENAVISTA

CALETA DE FUSTES

WESTERN CORDILLERA

CENTRAL PLAIN

EASTERN CORDILLERA

COASTAL PLAIN

Section A-B   1:200,000

swathe, sweeps up the eastern side almost to the top; most of what remains—the western half of the body of the island—is taken up by another chain of 600m peaks. Squeezed between the two cordilleras is a long well-populated plain, on average 250m above sea-level, which fits its shape into the surrounding foothills; it communicates with the east coast by the *barrancos* cut through the eastern range. A great lava-field and its cones surface the centre of the plain, and an even larger lava-field covers most of the northern end of the island, and there are other smaller ones. Sand blankets the rest of the northern end, the whole of the isthmus which leads on to the southern peninsula and several other sizeable areas. There is no vegetation worth showing on the map.

GEOLOGICAL ORIGINS

Fuerteventura's present landscape, like that of the rest of the Canaries, is of predominantly volcanic aspect. The origins and evolution of the archipelago are at present under intensive investigation by both traditional field approaches and by new techniques such as refraction seismic investigation and palaeomagnetic survey. Since some very recent ideas have already been abandoned and also because work is still in progress, it is proposed to summarise both the long-established 'common-origin' theory of the older geologists and biologists and then to note modern conflicting evidence and the recent 'separate development' hypothesis.

The old school, its main worker being Hausen, proposed that at one time the area now covered by the archipelago was simply an underwater extension of the African continent. The oldest rocks known in the Canaries, a plutonic complex at the base of Fuerteventura's western cordillera, may have been a part of the ancient basement. Fuerteventura's plutonic complex has suffered a displacement which, since it is similar to the Hercynian tectonic which affected the Pre-Cambrian of the adjacent Sahara, was probably also of Hercynian age, or Late Carboniferous. After a long denudation phase, the Eocene saw the

12

beginning of immense basalt eruptions which covered the whole pre-archipelago area; since then, erosion in Fuerteventura has brought the old worn plutonic rocks to light again. Following the Eocene basalt eruptions, and in the Miocene, and again apparently connected with distant geological activity, the whole vast pre-archipelago mass simply began to break into pieces; by then at least some of the area was already above the sea and, probably as a result of temporary land connection with the African continent, holding land flora and fauna, to be described later. The present archipelago came eventually into being. Between Fuerteventura and Gran Canaria charts now mark an extensive sub-island, its summit only 23m below the surface. In the case of the eastern islands, Fuerteventura and Lanzarote, they are believed to have been still united with the African continent into the Pliocene; by that time the present channel between them and the African coast is supposed to have reached the state of a great river valley, the flow being southwards from a northerly end closed by land now reduced to the submarine Banco de la Concepción. At the same time eastwards-running tributaries to the great canyon, from the single Lanzarote-Fuerteventura landmass, were cutting deep valleys through the Eocene basalts. It is remnants of these basalts which now form the eastern mountain chain of Fuerteventura—a system of towering parallel spines which, at right angles to the sea, cover the length of the Africa-facing side of the island, though not quite reaching to the northern tip. The Eocene basalts, forming the whole of the southern peninsula, also reach up to and overlie the south end of the ancient western cordillera, the latter disappearing beneath them not far north of the isthmus.

Recent investigations, summarised by Rothe and Schmincke, have yielded evidence suggesting totally opposed origins for the archipelago and some modifications of its evolution. Primarily, investigation of the sea floor has shown an oceanic crust around all but Fuerteventura and Lanzarote; only the latter pair do in fact lie in an area of continental crust and can have begun as an extension of the African land-mass. Separate study of Gran

FUERTEVENTURA

Canaria has led to the proposing of an origin for it which was independent of the rest of the oceanic-crust sub-division, with the latter's other members still to be studied. Both results draw attention to the means by which the endemic flora and fauna spread to and through the five western isles, since land-bridges become much less likely; the recent workers suggest natural tree-rafts. Relating to Fuerteventura and Lanzarote there are further discoveries. Thus on the former's west coast there are now known to be some thousand metres of sedimentary deposits, exposed over 3km, said to be older even than the western cordillera's plutonic basement. Fossil ostrich-eggs, recently found on Lanzarote, support the theory of land-bridges or shallow straits between the eastern islands and Africa throughout most of the Tertiary. The separation of the two islands by the strait from the African coast, all three aligned NNE–SSW, has been put down to the forces which caused the similarly oriented fractures, dykes and volcanoes of various ages within the two islands. Further research can be counted on to give a clearer and more complete picture of Canary geology.

THE CENTRAL PLAIN

After climbing the length of one of the Pliocene tributary valleys, between its 600m knife-edged walls or *cuchillos*, the south-bound road from the capital comes abruptly onto the central plain, the island's keep. Minute details in the immense landscape, dusty white villages patch the flat red alluvium, with the occasional yellowing crop rising from a field of black ash; the crosses on the belfries of the little churches and the vanes of the wind-driven water-pumps thrust pleading silhouettes at the unresponsively arid sky. The venerable western cordillera, a line of fused peaks each about 650m above sea-level, parallels the long plain. Opposite, coming in from the African coast, are the butt-ends of several ridges of the chopped-up eastern massif: they fall abruptly and merge into the plain. Blocking the southern end, 12km away, stands the Caldera de Gairía, a black dominant volcanic cone.

14

THE LAST VOLCANOES

Mainly to be seen in the north and centre of the islands, the freshest-looking cones are the remains of a series of outpourings which brought Fuerteventura's volcanic activity to a close. Following the general outpouring of Eocene basalts, already described, there seems to have been a comparative calm in the Fuerteventura land-mass for some fifty million years, until—by now a separate island—it underwent a fresh series of eruptions from about the middle Pleistocene. The lavas of the first set of these, although extensive, have become much covered by alluvium; neither are their cones any longer remarkable. More striking are the very late Pleistocene outbursts, the last. Geologically, these were not at all long ago, say contemporary with the Last Glaciation in the north, and they may have continued into the Recent period, which began some ten thousand years ago. The cones of these last eruptions have a very fresh aspect, and the Caldera de Gairía is the finest. The jagged, yellow-lichened crater, 461m, is a good hundred metres across, with a breach to the south; its bowl, lined with lilac-tinged brown lava and ash, is enlivened by a few Meade-Waldo's chats, small black and white birds. The outer slopes of the cone are strewn with twisted purple slag and a few fish-type volcanic bombs. Beyond the crater's flanks starts the lava-field, so infertile and unfriendly as to seem a *malpaís* or badland even to the islanders.

The *malpaíses* are difficult to cross. There is no firm ground, just the delicately-piled brittle rocks; one has no idea how deep they go. Jagged heaps with sudden pits between. A grit-laden wind. Now and then a respite on a minute cone of black ash which is dotted with prostrate plants, or in a channel of red alluvium. In the clefts, where some decomposed stone has filtered, the euphorbia stalks erupt, pallid green, bulging, to combine with the lichens to turn the already fantastic Malpaís to a luminous, frightening greenish-black.

The central plain's badland, 50sq km in extent, surrounds four old volcanoes: Gairía, 461m, Laguna, 301m, Liria, 254m, Arra-

15

bales, 247m, black cones in a line 8km long. These badlands are the absolute antithesis to all pretty landscapes, to all nice views, the purgative to cleanse the bowels of the mind of a surfeit of neat, charming, picturesque, postcard beauty-spots. Primarily, they are daunting, which was probably why—harassed by pirates and *conquistadores*, by local and European slave-catchers—many Mahohs lived there, hoping for safety amongst and within the deep, blistered, broken-up lava. Even now, after a further five hundred years of use as a common pasture, tracks are negligible; it is quicker to walk round rather than through. Nothing has been altered or added since the craters last exploded, except for the tinge of luminous green. Only vultures live there. The colour, the texture, the crunching of the glossy lava underfoot, all stimulate, like the feel of rough woollen cloth after nylon, or of an earthenware dish after china, or of a palm basket after plastic. The *malpaíses* work on the mind until it becomes utterly absorbed. All other places seem insipid, pale—conquered.

Two sets of northern cones are thought contemporary with those of the central plain. In the middle of the island's northern half, dominating the village of La Oliva, stands the isolated Montaña Arena, 420m; *arena* here refers to gritty black ash, of which the cone is made. Still darkly malignant, its crater burst faces north. An older, reddish ridge, which has kept itself above the volcano's lava-field, all but joins the cone to the base of the nascent cordillera to the east, there off to a high start with the peak of Escanfraga, 531m.

Most of the NW corner of the island is covered by another lava-field, roughly the size of that on the central plain; in wave after wave the lava disappears out to sea as the land's end. The five or six cones stand, suckered to the *malpaís* like scarlet sea-anemones, on the lava's eastern margin. The traveller from La Oliva first reaches the remaining half of a wrecked crater, an almost-glowing red crescent which lies against the flank of Great Deep Crater, 272m; unbreached, lilac and red, this cone is rimmed by soaring arches of brown lava. Behind it comes Enchanted Crater, with bombs the size of wine-barrels. The

16

Page 17: (above) Puerto del Rosario, the capital. The old jetty with fish traps on the left; (below) Betancuria, the first capital and Europe's first colonial settlement. The nearest building is the school. Agave cacti in foreground and prickly pears around houses

Page 18: (above) Fustes, once important east coast anchorage. Limekiln on left, 18th century defence tower mid-background. The skeleton is a camel's; (below) Gairía crater with central plain beyond. Villages of Valles de Ortega and, further off, Antigua

slopes of Bayuyo, 268m, the next northwards, are claret-coloured, flecked by olive-green bushes and black caves, and about its breach lie small bread bombs and mauve scraps of glossy slag. Cooling, the lava in San Rafael's bowl has remained hummocked by the last massive bubbles, now lichened. From the rim of San Rafael one looks across the lava-field and the sound to the Lobos cone, 122m, a smouldering red at sunset—the end of the chain.

TRAVERTINE AND ALLUVIUM

In addition to the directly volcanic products, the island is surfaced in some places by a lime-yielding travertine and in others by a cultivable alluvium.

Much of the island is coated with the pale buff travertine, noted again in connection with the origin of the Mahoh people. The calcareous skin is very evident on the slopes of the western cordillera, for example. The description of Morocco's travertine by the traveller Maw, written a century ago, serves for Fuerteventura : a sheet-like covering of tufaceous crust rising over hill and valley and following all the undulations of the ground, the result probably of the intensive heat of the sun rapidly drawing up water charged with soluble carbonate of lime from the calcareous strata, and drying it layer by layer on the surface until an accumulation several feet thick has been produced. According to Hausen, the necessary climate—very hot and very wet alternately—probably occurred from time to time in the Pleistocene. The most recent Fuerteventura volcanoes are 'post-travertine', being free of it, and their lavas lying upon it. Travertine, no doubt redeposited, occurs on the faces and broken edges of many Mahoh potsherds. The lime-kilns of the travertine zone are all abandoned; there is a lime factory at Puerto del Rosario.

The fertility of the central plain is due to its colourful capping of what is thought to be the decomposed ash of past volcanic eruptions. This, and a wide chocolate-coloured band along the east coast—an erosion deposit, much of it the result of the weathering of the dominating eastern basaltic range—are the

B

agricultural lands of the island. Both soils, entirely lacking vegetation, are very much open to erosion by torrential rain and by the trade winds; in a few places there is encroachment by dune sand. Still, with so much fertile land and so little water, soil conservation can hardly be expected to interest the islanders.

SAND WASTES

The word *jable*, a corruption of the French *sable*, is the islanders' name for any of the sandy wastes of Fuerteventura. The Castilian *arena*, sand, and *arenal*, a sandy place, are locally more often used for volcanic 'sand', fine ash, as mentioned.

The Jable de Vigocho, some seven square kilometres in extent, covers the northern flank of a mountainous bulge in the western coastline. The unceasing northerly gale has decomposed the limestone and sandstone which forms a part of the coast hereabouts and, adding to it sea-eroded sand and the plentiful land-snail shells, has driven the white mixture southwards, up the mountainside to over 300m above sea-level. There the sand seems to have re-solidified. The underlying rock, protruding, broken up here and there, speckles and dirties the dazzling mountainside. Shallow erosion channels furrow the surface, taking the sand downwards again when it rains.

In the Jandía Jable, 60sq km, the map only shows sand, rising to 200m, for example at Sheep Water Height and at Horse Bones, and a track on the west. But the latter is abandoned due to perpetual sand-drift; drivers heard talking nervously about 'trying to get through' mean the track along the eastern, tourism-development shore, described later. Water sources are not pinpointed on the map, though the Jable, only 50 sea-miles from the Sahara, is a desert in miniature; the few trickles, hidden under stones against evaporation, may dry up in the droughts.

Playa del Viejo Rey, a vast Mahoh midden on its southern headland, begins the north-west coast of the Jable. Setting off southwards, the traveller soon finds the sand furrowed by a series of dazzlingly white gullies. Gradually the coast divides into three : a narrow breaker-splashed ledge of sandstone, a steep cliff, sometimes rocky, often faced with a slope of sand, and, up above, dunes cut through by shallow ravines, the latter ending with a drop down the cliff onto the ledge. The lizards become paler, even sandy, and race round and round the sea-spurges trying to find hiding-places. These scaly little plants only seem to grow in the *jables*; they are full of sticky white poison. The cliff edge is pocked with the ruins of huts, buried in the sand, probably Mahoh. Doubtless the inhabitants used the evasive springs : Three Stone Water, Sheep Spring, Agua Liques.

Occasionally a few grazing camels may be seen, but, as will be described later, the goats and sheep which once pastured there have recently been banished for having eaten a few young trees at one of the land-speculation beaches far away on the eastern coast. Wild life is rare too. In the brooding haze of an afternoon a flock of sand-grouse perhaps breaks its camouflage, to settle and utterly vanish a few minutes away along the cliffs. Nearing the Jandía massif, the writhing sharp-crested dunes become black-tinged, the bowls green-speckled with rest-harrows bearing yellow gorse-like flowers. Now and again a large lime-yellow wood-louse scuttles away across the sand. At length the traveller feels rock underfoot, he has reached the shade and springs of the rarely-visited West Jandía mountains.

THE JANDÍA PENINSULA

The Jandía massif is considered by the Spanish geologist Benítez Padilla to be half an immense crater, open towards the north-west; similar may be the formations of Fámara in Lanzarote, of Anaga and Las Cañadas in Tenerife, and of El Golfo in Hierro. The Jable dunes die away amongst the ravines which split the northern end of the half-circle of mountains.

The traveller who has reached the mountains along the western coast of the dunes and is considering his camp site has three immediate choices of water. There is a good spring in the cliff face at Punta Paloma, in the last dunes : requiring the descent of the near-vertical sand wall, with a drop into the breakers for those who overshoot the narrow spray-washed ledge where the water wells out, it is only recommended, as Olivia Stone would say, for those in good mental and physical health and who have practised games and riding in their youth, and is anyway inadvisable for ladies, who should make other arrangements. Secondly, there is Agua Tarajalillo, Tamarisk Water, in the bed of one of the first ravines, well known as *más amarga que la mar*, more bitter than the sea. No shrub but tamarisk, nor grass nor even green slime grows at such a spring, salty even for Fuerteventura; it supports only midges, not even the goats drink there. The third source comes with a marked change in the coastal geology: after a few *barrancos* have been crossed, there appears a red ash tuff shot through with spaced dykes of glossy basalt. The ravines would cut down through the consolidated ash at a fast pace but for the black dykes which, running parallel to the coast, or about NE–SW, have the effect of terracing the softer layer. An ascent of one of these ravines is alternately a walk up an almost level stretch of rosy ash followed by an often difficult climb up the smooth face of a dyke. In places, water held up in the porous ash is to be found seeping out of cracks near the base of a dyke, and one can dig a hole and collect this water. Perhaps the ash has some filtering effect for, although very salty, the water is just drinkable.

The sun rises over the rim of the massive crescentic mountain. In a rich, early light the pink ash with its black stripes looks edible, a barely-cooled eruption of fantasy nougat. Below it, like a sheet of rippling, bubbly glass, the sea hisses across the sand. Leaving the west coast to continue its curve to the southern tip and the hidden, hardly-populated Cofete, a track climbs eastwards amongst the massif's sheer rock faces; this route was used 'in the old days in the summer' when the women came over to make cheeses, milking the *guaniles*, the free roaming goats.

The populated, eastern side of Jandía divides into the 18km of tourism-development zone from Matas Blancas to the village of Morro Jable—also to be described later—and the region to the south of the latter, the land's end. This gale-swept tip is flat and desolate, the mountains having stopped well short of the sea. The only relief is the lighthouse and perhaps, in the distance, a few goats. The coast disappears under the sea as a series of reefs, the hunting-ground of the melancholy, hunched turnstone.

FOSSIL SHORELINES

In addition to the land-building volcanic activity, the island's area has been alternately increasing and decreasing as a result of changes in the height relationship of land and sea. The most distinctive of Fuerteventura's ancient shorelines is that now at 15 to 18m above sea-level. The melting of the ice in the north, during the last interglacial period, was responsible for a world rise in sea-level; its upper shoreline, traced, for example, in London, Gibraltar and the Marmora Sea, is known as the First Monastirian.

In Fuerteventura the relic is a conspicuous feature of the west coast, notably just below the top of the El Cangrejo cliffs, nearest Santa Inés. The shoreline terrace is surfaced with a thin layer of eroding brown sandy stone. This is thickly studded with bleached fossil shells, contrasting with the massive glittering middens of modern shellfish eaters spread along the cliff edge above. The most common fossil shells are probably a large barnacle (*Tetraclita squamosa*) and the Portuguese oyster (*Crassostrea angulata*). Both are living species and Fuerteventura is within their present range of distribution, though they seem not to occur on the present coast.

In the Canaries, according to Zeuner, the First Monastirian is the earliest of three clear Late Pleistocene terraces. Otherwise, going upwards in height and backwards in time, the islands hold other less common and less well understood terraces—one, for example, at some 80m up. The earliest and highest of all is now at about 100m above sea-level : it marks a shoreline of the Miocene period, roughly the time at which, according to the old school of geologists, the pre-archipelago mass was splitting up

23

into islands. An example of this terrace is well known in Gran Canaria, and Hausen has noted traces of the same sea in the north of Fuerteventura, south-east of Los Lajares. Hausen also mentions a report by a Spanish geologist, Hernández Pacheco, that, amongst the several ancient shorelines to be seen on the West African coast, there is one between 10 and 12m above present sea-level; amongst the deposits related to this have been found semi-fossilised mollusc shells and stone tools of Acheulean type.

But neither Fuerteventura nor any of the other islands have yielded human traces in association with ancient shoreline relics, and there is no reason to suppose that they ever will. It does not seem to have been easy for early animals of any kind to reach the archipelago; for much of the time the islands must have been too volcanically active to be tempting. Zeuner has suggested two waves of arrivals, the first probably in Miocene-Pliocene times, the second, comparatively not long ago, around the Pleistocene-Recent border. Caught up dead or alive by volcanic material and fossilised, there have been found giant rats, their species apparently not yet decided, giant lizards (*Lacerta goliath, L. maxima*), tortoises or turtles (*Testudo burchadii*), ostrich and other birds' eggs and an unknown vertebrate bone; add to this group the probable presence of such still-surviving curiosities as the islands' laurel and dragon trees, and an earwig—their nearest relatives now respectively in the East Indies, Madagascar, and China—plus the Canaries' unique blue chaffinch, and one has a very slight idea of the early aspect of the islands, for these were probably all first-wave arrivals. Three shrubs, *Euphorbia canariensis, E. handiensis, Kleinia neriifolia*, all described in the course of this book, are to be seen at their best on Fuerteventura; they are limited to the archipelago and may also be of very early implantation. Of the fossil forms, only the giant lizards have descendants today (*Lacerta simonyi s., L.s.stehlini*); the size of these modern species is no less than 60–70cm, but another species, twice as long, existed until fairly recently. Of course, most of the first flora and fauna has certainly disappeared without leaving any fossil trace.

24

LANDSCAPE

The only fossil mammal found is the huge rat, an undistinguished beginning for the archipelago; but, when it comes to being transported upon a drifting tree trunk, a rat is more likely to cross than an elephant, and it is probable that this was at least one of the means by which land-forms reached the islands.

Fuerteventura and Lanzarote, apparently joined longer to the African continent than were the rest, may perhaps hold a land fauna and flora slightly different from those of the other islands; *Euphorbia handiensis*, for instance, is in fact limited to a few specimens in the Jandía. The Mahoh middens, so far unreported, may yield bones of extinct fauna. Present larger land-bound species are no more than cistern-dwelling frogs, small lizards including the gecko, the usual mice and rats, rabbits in the dunes and, so it is said, hedgehogs in the ruins and stone-clearance heaps of the central plain. In the backwoods of Ibiza, in the Balearics, the author has seen hedgehogs bred in pits for eating, so even this animal may have been brought into Fuerteventura recently. Specialists could examine the various species for 'living fossils'.

In the Jandía there is a Valle del Ciervo, Deer Valley. Could any foundation for the name be located, it would certainly enliven the island's animal record.

2 NATURAL HISTORY

IT is probably a long time since the Canaries were the paradise garden of the burgeoning tourist brochures. The last major African pluvial phase, in the Late Pleistocene and thought to have ended about 10,000 B.C., would presumably have seen the island rather greener than its present barren self. For the last time, the Tertiary-origin tributaries through the eastern cordillera would have been streams in their own right. Many species of plants and animals, having crossed on the already broken Tertiary land-bridge, and today extinct, would have shared the island with those which have clung on until the present, thought to be mainly Late Pleistocene arrivals. Yet other species must have come and gone with the pluvial period. Compared with this wet phase which ended some 12,000 years ago, the climate since has been generally drier, although there have been lesser fluctuations. It is probable that the island was already a potential desert, with easily extinguished vegetation and wildlife, when men first arrived on it. And only another major pluvial will make Fuerteventura a tolerably easy place to live, let alone a garden of delights.

CLIMATE

There are three climatic zones: the shore, the central plain, the mountains. To a northern traveller, the two lower, those now inhabited, are at their best in the winter. Then the shoreline, though hot, is not unpleasantly so, and the nights are cool; the eastern coast is often windless, though the western is incessantly attacked by gales. In the summer the shores are calm and hot, the atmosphere oppressive. The naked central plain is scoured for much of the year by a strong dust-laden wind; in winter the plain varies between cool and warm, becoming in summer as hot and, when the wind ceases, as airless as the shorelines. The mountain zone is pleasantest on a hot windy summer's day; in winter the powerful wind becomes icy, and ever ready, if cloud level falls to the summits, to turn into a chilling misty gale. The rare rain, torrential as becomes an island of extremes, is best witnessed from a vantage point overlooking the central plain : the vast clouds, black and rolling with thunder, are here and there joined to the red, darkening earth by swiftly-moving columns of grey rain. The intervening droughts often last three years, during which 15–20cm will be the total rainfall.

VEGETATION

Botanists should visit the island soon after it has rained, but before its 1700sq km of awoken plant life have been nibbled away by the relentless flocks. Most of the vegetation now described, with the further plants in Appendix 1, is significantly inedible to goats. The description begins with the shore plants and, in roughly rising order, ends on the mountain summits.

On Isla Lobos, perhaps because of its isolation, there grows a plant which does not exist on Fuerteventura itself; around its marshy salt-water lagoon lives *espinocho*, an odd sea-lavender (*Limonium ?papillatum*, hybrid), papery lilac and white flowers on green stems.

Opposite, the main island's Jable del Moro, like the other sand-wastes behind the shores, also supports a peculiar, perennial vegetation. Five species, relieving the glare of the dunes and sheltering snails and the lizards, are seen at their best there : the bulbous green and orange leaves of the little *barbosa* (*Zygophyllum fontanesii*), also known in the centre of the island as *cosco macho*, the snaking monkeypuzzle-like green arms of the milky sea-spurge (*Euphorbia paralias*), the little gorse-flowered rest-harrow (*Ononis natrix*, sub-sp. *hispanica* var. *canariensis*),

27

the mournful grey-green clumps of the orache *salado* (*Atriplex parvifolia*), the camel-fodder *yerba mora*, a seablite, which forms huge green bushes which turn a warm red as they mature (*Suaeda vermiculata*).

The natural route up from the shore is to climb the boulder-strewn bed of a *barranco*, picking a way up a watercourse furrowed by ancient spates. Nothing can be expected to grow on the surface of the deep hot stones, yet suddenly the eye is startled to find, just ahead, the detested colocynth (*Citrullus* [*Cucumis*] *colocynthis*). The little round gourds, purest of yellows, spread amongst the gravel and pebbles of the watercourse, jostled by younger dark green specimens and crushing their ancient browning ancestors; nothing is said to touch them, though some looked to have been picked out, as by a bird. Inside there are layers of a felt-like pulp which encases large brown pips, and the gourd gives off a bitter odour. It has a long history in the preparation of purgatives, and organised cultivation in Fuerteventura would be possible; in fact, if present northern trends towards refinement of foods and a sedentary life continue, colocynth plantations might well add considerably to the island's economy. The gourd is ideally adapted to Fuerteventura, for it always seems to be growing upon banks of gravel in the hottest, most barren places.

The coastal ravines usually have their heads in the central plain or its rambling extensions north to La Oliva and south to Gran Tarajal; at much the same height, down behind the western cordillera, lies the Río Palmas valley. In this zone, of medium height and running on up into the lower slopes of the cordilleras and other mountains, there can be found the majority of the island's species; though many extend to the height extremes, they grow as well in the middle zone as anywhere.

Strangely, the wide-spread shrub which at once catches the eye, perhaps because it is the most tree-like, is probably a nineteenth-century arrival and native to Brazil: the slender, drooping *mimus* or tree tobacco (*Nicotiana glauca*). It yields only tomato canes and, to the disgust of the islanders—who also call

28

it *venenero*, poisoner, and *tabaco moro*, Moor's tobacco—
hybridises with their true tobacco plants. The shrub often
reaches 4 to 5m high, a swaying dark green form now at home
on Fuerteventura.

Possibly the most interesting of the island's native plants, the
four euphorbias are certainly its most repellent; this accounts for
their survival. As numerous as the *mimus* but less immediately
striking, the notorious *tabaiba* (*E. regis-jubae*) is shunned by men
and goats; usually about a metre high, a short thick grey stem
from which rise pudgy brown arms bearing a canopy of long
thin pointed pale green leaves, it is allowed to develop into a well
shaped bush. Two cactus-like euphorbias are *E. handiensis*, limited
to the Jandía, and *E. canariensis*, the *cardón*, in Fuerteventura
perhaps restricted to the eastern slope of Monte Cardón. The discovery in the island of the latter species by Euphorbus, physician
to King Juba II, led to the whole family being named after him;
as will be explained, the event is also an important piece of
evidence in the dating of the Canaries' first main human immigration. This euphorbia grows in dense groups, to a height of
two metres. Each slender stem is ribbed, or flanged, vertically :
five ridges, five angles, so that in cross-section they would
be rather like a five-pointed star. Spikes grow in pairs all the
way down the ridges. New green stems seem able to bud
from any point on the old ones; the latter eventually turn grey
and die.

All three species, together with the dunes' *E. paralias*, break at
a touch and drip a sticky white venom. This is so poisonous that
the islanders collect the milk in bottles and pour it into the sea,
into a big rock-pool, for example, and the fish all die or go mad,
and rise to the surface, to be picked out by the fishermen; in fact,
with various plants, this has long been done on the Spanish peninsula too. Euphorbia milk, which the eighteenth-century voyager
Captain Glas suggested would serve for pitching boats, has many
island uses : for example, whitening boundary stones, snaring
birds, sealing up udders to stop the lambs and kids from feeding.
The word *tabaiba*, like *tobobo* for hoopoe, is probably of pre-

conquest origin, and so probably are several of the uses for the white juice.

Easily confused with the *tabaiba*, with which it consorts, is another common shrub, peculiar to the Canaries : *Kleinia neriifolia*. This, *berol*, is kept stripped by the goats, and at a glance resembles a disfigured *tabaiba* but for its more bulgy greyer arms and for its lack of white juice. Better defended but chewed nevertheless are the zone's lizard sanctuaries, the crouched porcupine-like grey thorn-bushes, the *aulaga* (*Launaea spinosa*). Miguel de Unamuno, the Spanish poet and philosopher, exiled to Fuerteventura throughout the spring of 1924 by Primo de Rivera's government, wrote enthusiastically of the *aulaga* flower, which is something like a half-closed yellow daisy; in another work, more usually forgotten, a catalogue of Fuerteventura's blemishes included *flores sin olores*, scentless flowers. Another prickly shrub is *espárrago* (*Asparagus alba*), its long arms straggling across the many ruins of the plain. A third spiky bush, *espino* (*Lycium afrum*), is able to grow in the lava-fields, where there is little else but lichens and *tabaibas*.

Other than the *mimus*, none of these shrubs is of remarkable beauty, Unamuno's *aulaga* no more than the rest. Dried for fodder, the *cebollina* (*Asphodelus microcarpus*) is comparatively rare. At the moment when the sun, first appearing over the eastern *buttes*, floods the plain with light, here and there the slopes of tall asphodels become incandescent, lines of unimportant candles in a dazzlingly lit landscape.

A dozen species have played various useful, often vital roles in the island's economy, and will be fully described; they include lichens, glassworts, prickly pears, an agave, a thistle, a thyme, a truffle and the sun-rose.

Truly wild trees probably do not exist, but the traveller occasionally sees a cypress or a pine amongst the produce trees near a farm. The island's botanical garden—fed by a well of pure water—is probably the dense uncared-for orchard below the ancient farm of 'El Cortijo Antiguo', on the Antigua face of the western cordillera; its architecture is to be described later.

The trees and shrubs stretch along the *barranco* bed. Old grey figs, gigantic evergreen carobs, wild clumps of pale tamarisk, guava trees, their bark smooth and coffee-coloured, a few decrepit quinces with grape vine straggling along the terrace around them, some Canary palms, almond trees in flower, pomegranates, bitter orange bushes, aspens everywhere, a tall cypress being prepared to yield a roof beam and, just on the other side of the watercourse, two turpentine trees, perhaps the last on the island, and beside them a wild olive. But the eye-catching tree, which stands freely where one can take it in, is a dragon, said to be the only one on Fuerteventura.

The dragon (*Dracaena draco*), a *Liliaceae* survival from the Mesozoic era—and probably a Tertiary arrival in the Canaries—would be really rather a comic tree, if one could only see it shorn of its legendary atmosphere, or if it were common. Its odd appearance had become known in Europe by the sixteenth century, for Hieronymous Bosch included it in the 'Garden of Delights'; one can believe that the tree appealed to that painter's fantasy-orientated imagination. The dragon, then, has a thick straight trunk covered in warty grey elephant skin; at a height of two or three metres, not high enough in proportion to its fat trunk, so that it is a stumpy tree, it suddenly divides into about a dozen quite bare sausage-like arms; these rise for a metre or so and then, after dividing again with mathematical precision, disappear into an untidily ruffled and yet quite charming dense crown of thin green strips. These strips, up to 50cm long and tapering to a point, like green paper streamers, spill and spread in all directions, growing somehow on the hidden tops of the sausage-like arms. The dense vivid green upon the pale grey, with a patch of the darkest shadow on the ground below, make a fresh, cool sight even amongst the other trees. And, in addition to its odd appearance, the dragon has blood-red pith and, some say, lives a thousand years. That at El Cortijo Antiguo, which grows date-like sprays of small berries in its unruly crest, is thought to be at least that old.

Leaving the level of the alluvium plain and climbing the stony ravines towards the cordilleras' summits, one finds the vegetation thinning. Colonies of squills, *cebollas albarranas* (*Urginea maritima*), thrive on the damp north-facing slopes; the fat, rather smug bulbs, interred up to their waists, each sport a few big glossy green pointed leaves. Amongst the ruins of the pre-conquest Risco del Carnicero peak settlement the tiny vulture's cactus, *tunera de guirre* (*Caralluma burchardii*), grows as nowhere else; from the tips of the clustered fingers, grey and ribbed, sprout pairs of purplish antennae, each feeler 8–10cm long. Perhaps the island's exquisite plant occurs right on the summit of the western cordillera. With the Morro de la Cruz the range turns westwards and, on the northern flank of the peak, amongst a stepped chaos of grey rocks delicately tinted with strap-shaped lemon-coloured lichens (*Ramalina bourgeana*), the climber will find a scattering of silver-grey bushes which bear round golden flowers, clusters of minute suns. Spared by the goats, these are called *jorado* (*Asteriscus sericeus*).

Trees on the cordilleras would encourage rain to fall and for this reason the mountains containing the Río Palmas valley have been planted with pines by the state. *Pinus canariensis* has three long needles to a cluster, which gives it a hairier aspect than that of northern species. Unfortunately, the habitat in its present state seems too severe for the trees, and the plantations are sadly patchy, with many of the pines dwarfish.

Land reclamation, past and present, has always had opposition : the shepherds. In the eighteenth century, even the Lord of Fuerteventura was short-sighted or self-interested enough to forbid the ploughing of animal pastures. Within living memory the shepherds around La Oliva, in the north, have wrecked a pine plantation, pulling every tree out of the ground in the night. To the shepherds, trees are often planted so that, when the goats are caught eating them, there has to be compensation; this is enforced if necessary by the Civil Guard. Another reactionary attitude is common. For example, the agricultural experts planted a few experimental tree-heaths (*Erica arborea*) in one of the cordillera ravines, for they do well in Tenerife, though

32

a little higher above sea-level. The farmer later remarked: 'Who were they to come and tell me, when I've lived in this valley all my life, what to plant here?' He said the heaths had all died and was clearly pleased. Pessimism and ignorance feed each other in Fuerteventura, a vicious circle which—like drought and lack of vegetation—it is not easy to break up.

BIRDS

Of the ninety-seven species (see Appendix 2) recorded on Fuerteventura, thirty-eight at least have bred there. The common birds fall into two rough groups, those which live in the most deserted regions and those at home around the farm buildings and fruit trees.

The first ornithological notes on Fuerteventura are the French conquerors': '. . . very rich in birds, in herons, bustards, river birds with unusual plumage, big pigeons with white-edged tails, and ordinary ones, so many that it's unbelievable, but the falcons kill them all, and quails, larks and numberless others; and some birds which are big and white like a goose, and are always amongst the people and don't leave any filth'. Unlikely to be already known to the northerners, the last species is clearly the Egyptian vulture; now becoming rarer, it has until recently been the winged garbage-disposal unit of the towns and villages of the Canaries. Its name, *guirre*, is listed by Glas as amongst the speech of the ancient inhabitants of La Palma—the one island where it has never been recorded. Though present on Fuerteventura, it is not numerous. Most majestic of Fuerteventura's birds, this black and white vulture can often be seen spiralling above the central plain.

However, of those independent species which live out in the island's deserts, the most attuned to the naked landscape are the sand-brown plain-dwellers: the little courser, the thick-knee, the large houbara bustard. Perfectly blended with the earth and rock, only a chance encounter forces one to move and fly a few metres. It lands and vanishes. The walker marks the spot and

33

goes towards it, but the bird is not there, either due to a mis-judgement or because it has scuttled away unnoticed amongst the rocks and runnels; in each case saved by its camouflage.

The more domesticated birds will be found at their most con-centrated in the overgrown ravine described in the last section, a haven which even after three years' drought is green and shady. This bird sanctuary is dominated by shrikes. Their favourite position here, for lack of the tip of a vane of an abandoned wind-mill, is the tops of the aspens, where they glisten like the creamy-grey backs of the leaves. Their voice is a high-pitched grinding, then, after a pause, a lower note : pprrrrr . . . iiipp. They sit there, outlined against the mountains on the further side of the plain, until suddenly one of them throws itself off and into a long skim-ming dive which takes it down into the thick coppice along the watercourse; there the beetles and other insects are plentiful. The local people respect the shrike and call him 'a noble bird'. He is master of the ravine, splendid in his grey and black plumage and long tail, the black mask suiting his piratical life.

A buzzing like a busy switchboard, followed by two or three squeaks. On the corner of a terrace, the trumpeter bullfinch, like a minute pink parrot, twists its head over to look down. The grotesquely-huge red beak opens, and he buzzes again. Amongst the cultivation weeds there are six or seven more, busily hunting for seeds. Alerted, they are invisible, pinkish-brown against the dusty red earth. Abruptly, amidst a flutter of black and white wings, a prowling shrike passes across them and all dive for the thicket of pomegranate trees around the well. Once or twice a faint, indignant buzz can be heard.

The hoopoes are as timid as the shrikes are masterful. This feminine bird's body is the colour of a ripe peach, and on top of its slender head it has a crest tipped with black and white; at the slightest alarm the crest ripples open and erect, the hoopoe sometimes jumping into the air in fright. When not squabbling nor oop-oop-ooping from some vantage point, the hoopoe's main occupation is that of probing the ground with its long fine beak, after worms and grubs. The colour of the earth, the bird is hard

34

Page 35: (above) Windward coast, Jandía, at low tide, looking south from Agua Tarajalillo; (below) Basalt dykes in pink ash tuff, near Agua Tarajalillo

Page 36: (above) Playa del Vieyo Rey, west coast. Jandía Wall in middle distance. Highest background is Monte Cardón, 593 metres; (below) The fortified summit of Monte Cardón

to spot—until it breaks into its dipping butterfly-like flight, when the big black and white wings betray it even at a distance.

Others birds appear and disappear. Occasionlly a fat stripy snipe stands pensively on a heap of branches which have fallen into the water tank; perhaps it is waiting for the last few inches to evaporate so as to catch the frogs. Turtle-doves, in the tamarisks, keeping up their idiotic bird-bleating all day long. Cabrera's blackbirds, nesting. A drowned kestrel in the tank, perhaps after the frogs; and the vigilant ravens are diving and swooping above the spot. Sparrows, the males with bright white cheeks, roistering about in the palm trees. And always the minute tits, the *alegría*, or 'happiness', as the shepherds call them, the smallest of the Canaries' four sub-species : singing, hopping about the *mimus* shrub, picking out the pomegranates, hurtling yellow, blue and black images which disappear into holes in the walls.

Generally, the Fuerteventura birds, almost the only wild life, are decreasing in quantity. There are many reasons. Less tree cover, less edible vegetation, usually no water for 'river birds'. The competition of ornithologists and 'oologists' for the rarer eggs; whilst cursing each other for past depredations, they continue to collect nevertheless. One expert felt the increasingly rare Fuerteventura houbara bustard—peculiar to the island—to be best served by taking the clutches of eleven nests in a few days; others shoot the birds in the hope of finding a freakish specimen or an unnamed 'sub-species'. The island children, when not in the service of the egg-hunters, usually trample on the nests, or did so in the past. Organised parties of sportsmen now come to hunt from outside; the black-bellied sandgrouse, in the Canaries limited to Fuerteventura, is a particular target, and the author saw only one or two groups. The heron, anyway extremely rare, is safe at least from the islanders, since it is thought that to shoot it will bring bad luck, but otherwise the hungry people shoot or snare everything edible, for kindness to animals and the preservation of wild life are the luxuries of those who have plenty to eat.

c

INSECTS

Few places actually rear insects by the million, but this Fuerteventura has done for a century and a half : the cochineal bug and industry will be described later. More domesticated still, in decreasing order of quantity, are the flies and mosquitoes, the cockroaches, which can reach huge size (Madeiran species), and the blackbeetles. Midge attacks occur in the vicinity of the west coast's salty springs. Not noisome and rather more interesting are the large yellow woodlice of the dunes and the trapdoor spiders in the central plain alluvium.

SHORE AND SEA

Shellfish, which have always played an important part in the food-gathering island community, must once have been more common than they are today. The ancient middens include the shells of huge limpets (*Patella oculus*). The modern shell-heaps are mainly composed of the purplish-silver mussel *Perna perna*, its shells up to 14cm long. The Mahohs also collected a species of *Conus*, grinding their flat necklace plaques out of the curving wall. Perhaps the beaches with most shells are those in the Lanzarote sound.

Sea-cucumbers and sea-centipedes creep about the inshore reefs. Judged underwater, the commonest of the larger fish of the shallows is seen to be the fat and torpid red wrasse, endemic. The all but inedible and utterly lethargic trumpet-fish, tube-like, with a minute dorsal fin set down near the tail and spotted with electric blue, drifts hither and thither; there are perhaps a few dozen to each bay. The occasional barracudas rather resemble the trumpet-fishes, but are harder to approach, departing like erratic torpedoes into the foggy distance. Groupers, greener than in the Mediterranean, are in fact few. Local fishermen say tunny come inshore when rounding the southern tip. There is a high proportion of notorious species. The moray and a larger yellow eel, whose interests clash. Sting-rays are common, reaching

38

several metres overall. A hammer-head shark, eyes out on the end of its T-shaped cranium, sometimes circuits a bay. As close in as they can get without being rolled about, the squatting malignant weavers squint upwards; they have poisonous dorsal spines, and are quite common. Deeper water species can be studied in the market.

3   PREHISTORY

THERE is much about the archipelago's first people which still eludes archaeologists. Not that their daily life, at least that of the conquest time, is unknown: several eye-witnesses record it, though sketchily and sometimes contradictorily. It is the prehistory of the Mahohs and of the other islands' populations—like the Guanches of Tenerife—which is still confused. When did the first settlers arrive and from where? And in what sort of boats? What physical type of people were they, and what language did they speak? Did they bring with them the way of life that the conquerors found, or did one or perhaps several more immigrant waves each superimpose its own culture? To what extent did each island have a distinct prehistory? Was there really no regular communication between one and the other, with the knowledge of ship-making really lost? Finally, and perhaps most interesting of all, what impelled people to cross to the islands in the first place? Some of these questions have been answered in part, others not at all.

PRE-CONQUEST ISLANDERS

The more or less factual side, as opposed to the theoretical, is easily enough summarised; unfortunately there is no locally excavated information by which to divide up the Canaries' ancient people chronologically or into cultural groups, so that Fuerteventura's prehistory is still unseparated from that of the archipelago in general. The bulk of the pre-conquest Canary islanders fell into two types, one with a wide, robust face, the other's tall and narrow. By modern world standards, the majority

40

of the men were of medium height, the women rather above. The colour of the skin, hair and eyes varied considerably. Their blood was about 90% in the O group. They kept short-haired unevolved-Mamber goats and possibly others resembling the screw-horned Jericho breed, unevolved slender-Mediterranean pigs, medium-sized dogs resembling dingos and another breed similar but with a broader face and hanging ears; some dialects at least had words for sheep and the conquerors reported seeing them but, though sheep and goat bones are often hard to tell apart, archaeologists claim to find only the latter. Rotary querns in all islands, words in their language for barley, and some of the conquest-time descriptions, together put beyond doubt that all islands had some knowledge of agriculture; some sound as if they grew wheat as well as barley. They ate meat and grain, milk, butter and cheese, and great quantities of shellfish, and also fruit, fish and flour made of roots; they dried and stored their food in hollow conical cairns. Most early descriptions say skins or vegetable fabrics were worn, one or two refer to the people as going naked; some mention footwear, others headgear.

They did not spin or weave, but they did both flat and spiral plaiting with vegetable materials, including a sedge grass. They did not have metal objects. Their stone industries were of great importance to them, but extremely crude and generally without a trace of specialised technique; quite uncharacteristic are four polished axes. They also made tools out of wood, bone and shell. Some are said to have produced fire by rubbing two sticks together; others used a wooden drill in a dried thistle; no reference of fire was recorded. Their pots were very varied; craftsman-wise, the most primitive were those resembling truncated ostrich eggs, known both plain and with incised decorations; the most evolved had the shapes and perhaps even imitated the hammer marks of metal pots, and bore painted geometrical patterns; they knew burnishing but not glazing; on one island lids were carved out of travertine. Many small clay dies, each with a different pattern, have been found in one island. They did not have ships nor did they know navigation at the time of the conquest; fishing was in the shallows. Some lived in caves, some dug dwellings into the ground, some lived in stone huts, round, rectangular, bayed, and some cross-shaped; there is no sign that they ever had tents.

Scantily-recorded, their speech, with both similarities and differences between islands, was not exactly any known tongue past or present; much of it is of untraced origin, but it did include many words which occur in the Berber spoken at present on the adjacent continent and, though the extent of their usage is not known, a few Arabic words; in one island there was, and still is, a whistled second language. The people were apparently analphabetic at the time of the conquest; undeciphered inscriptions have been found cut into the rocks; some, like the spirals, were not alphabetic, others were undoubtedly a form of writing; some of the latter are comparable to the Saharan Tifinagh inscriptions, the work of past and present Berber-speakers.

Kingship and hierarchies of nobles, matriarchy and patriarchy, all were known, varying with the island. A despised caste existed around a few occupations. Polyandry and bride-fattening were practised in at least one island; for another, there is both a suggestion of a fourteenth-century fertility cult and a report that, long before the conquest and because of a chronic state of famine, it was decreed that all female children, other than the first born, should be killed at birth; both the lord's right of the first night and also wife-loan to honour strangers were reported. The central religious belief of the majority was in a single supreme being; varying with the island, the religions included a male and female deity, heavens, worship of the sun, moon and stars, spirits of ancestors, a devil which could take the form of a dog, a pig which could intercede in time of trouble; a few idols have been found, some of dogs and pigs, others of the Mediterranean 'violin-shaped' type; food offerings were made; some had priests, others had male or female prophets; worship was in special buildings, in caves or on mountains. Embalming and mummification, simpler than that of the Egyptians, were practised in some islands; the dead were buried singly or communally, in caves or in the ground, in the latter case sometimes under tumuli; sometimes with a vessel of food, sometimes with a dog.

They fought with throwing stones—one island used slings—and wooden spears, including a type with a pommel made of two balls, and, at close quarters, with stone knives, wooden swords and round wooden shields; both civil war and duelling to rules occurred. Some decorated themselves with clay beads, some with small rectangular shell plaques. They sang and danced but no musical instrument has been found or recorded; they wrestled and played athletic games. Meetings for common purposes were held in prepared assembly grounds. In character they were resolute and honest, and their justice was severe. Towards their foes they were magnanimous and trusting.

The lengthy and circumstantial descriptions of the ancient people of Gran Canaria, Tenerife and La Palma, telling how they behaved both in peace and in the defence of their islands, show that far from being 'savages'—which, for most if not all of their contemporaries rationalised everything that was done to them—many aspects of their social order and personal conduct can bear any comparison, and on average their standards were perhaps rather higher than those of Medieval Europe.

ORIGIN OF ISLANDERS

Most of these facts do not of course help to reconstruct the origins of the pre-conquest people. But a sketch of the possible significance of the more peculiar material can be attempted.

Archaeology shows that 'tool-making hominids' roamed Africa as long ago as the Pliocene, a period which ended at least a million years ago and the one during which Fuerteventura and Lanzarote were last united to the continent; no trace of any such pre-men has so far been found in any of the Canaries. Next, it is quite certain that, during the succeeding Pleistocene, tool-makers were abundant on the nearby continent; but even by the end of this period, ten or twelve thousand years ago, the fifty sea-miles between Fuerteventura and the African coast had apparently still not been crossed by man, as the hominids can now be called.

It is probable that, following the end in about 10,000 BC of the last major African pluvial phase, the human population of the Sahara began to migrate in all directions, forced to do so by the effects of the increasing dryness upon supplies of game and plants. Apparently soon after 10,000 BC and in the region of Jericho, the world's first agriculture began; one direction in which the knowledge spread was westwards along the North African coast. By about 4000 BC it was taking root at the western end of the Mediterranean coast. At this time in this area the members of a group of pre-Neolithic people, whose culture is known to archaeology as 'Upper Capsian', were superimposing themselves upon another and more stagnant pre-Neolithic group of 'Oranian' culture; by 3000 BC the latter were eliminated from the coastal zone, many probably retreating into indefinite survival in refuge zones such as the Atlas mountains. The result of the blending of the knowledge of agriculture with a people of strongly-marked Capsian cultural ancestry was the Neolithic-of-Capsian tradition culture which, spreading down even to the Congo, lasted at least into the period 2000–1000 BC and, in the hinterlands, probably longer.

The Oranians' physique, closely related to the Cro-Magnon, included a distinctive, rather primitive face—wide, with prominent brow ridges—and has been named the 'Mechta-Afalou' type; the Capsians, who had tall, narrow faces, were 'Early Mediterraneans'. It is now accepted that the bulk of the pre-conquest islanders were descended from these two physical groups. Rather less agreed is the order and time of their arrival in the archipelago, and the following reconstruction of this aspect is only the author's opinion.

The only coherent classical account of the Canary Islands, that in Pliny, was taken from a description by the expeditionaries of King Juba II; his long reign, most of the time over the Roman protectorate of Mauretania, covered the year of the birth of Christ. The expedition left a detailed account of the islands' endemic *cardones*, and these plants' family, the euphorbias, has since been named after King Juba's physician, Euphorbus. According to Pliny, this not-unintelligent-sounding expedition reported that the Canaries were then uninhabited. However, two islands bore signs of past human life: 'Canaria' has *vestigia aedificiorum*, of 'Junonia' Pliny wrote: *in ea aediculam esse tantum lapide extructam.* A dwelling or two for Phoenician orchil collectors and goat hunters, the shacks of the victims of a shipwreck, a fisherman who had drifted across on the one-way current from the continent—these are all possibilities. Long before being finally settled, many islands all over the world were no doubt intermittently occupied by a variety of humans, most of whom disappeared without a trace. There are many reasons for accepting the validity of the Juba account, as will be shown.

Juba reigned from 29 BC to about AD 20. Mauretania, including the present Morocco, was made into a Roman province in AD 42. During the Romans' domination of North Africa their harsh attitude over taxes provoked the Berber-speaking inhabitants to repeated revolts; raids from the unsubjected areas were also frequent. In AD 100, for example, there had to be a punitive expedition against the Teda of the Tibesti mountains. Banishment, a common Roman punishment, was one way of dealing with rebellious tribes . . . and Juba II's description of the uninhabited Canaries, then the south-western corner of the known world, would have been to hand. In Glas there is a quotation from Galindo who himself took it, in 1632, from a more ancient work:

'when Africa was a Roman province, the natives of Mauretania rebelled, and killed their Presidents and Governors; upon which the senate, resolving to punish and make a severe example of the rebels, sent a powerful army into Mauretania, which vanquished and reduced them again to obedience; soon after, the ring-leaders of the rebellion were put to death; and the tongues of the common sort, and of their wives and children, were cut out, and then they were all put on board vessels, with some grain and cattle, and transported to the Canary Islands.'

45

This may be somebody's speculation, but it is oddly circumstantial, and to it one can add that the 1402 French chroniclers wrote of the Gomerans, many of whom use a finger-aided *articulated* whistling language—of a unique construction, according to Classe—in addition to Castilian, that 'they say there that a great prince for no crime had them put into exile there, and had their tongues cut out'. If one accepts for the moment these two apparently independent reports—and, even if one stems from the other, it nevertheless remains that some such tradition did exist—the date of arrival of the ancestors of the conquest time islanders can thus be placed between the death of Juba II in AD 20, or, rather, the annexation of Mauretania by the Romans, in AD 42, and AD 429, when, falling to the Vandals, Africa ceased to be 'a Roman province'. And, of about a dozen radiocarbon datings recently carried out on the earliest-looking dateable archaeological specimens in the Canaries, the earliest date given was AD 290±60. So the ancestors of the conquest time islanders may well have appeared in the archipelago during the first few centuries after Christ.

Taking this, the Mauretanian exiles theory, as a working basis, the rest of the evidence can be reviewed. The most valuable is that of physical types, the only aspect of Canary archaeology sufficiently studied. Recent anthropological work suggests that, evolutionarywise, between the primitive 'Mechta-Afalous' and 'Early Mediterraneans' of North Africa of, say, roundabout 3000 BC, and the first islanders' physiques, there is a big gap, much greater than that between the latter and the representatives of those physiques amongst the twentieth-century islanders and North Africans. The first islanders were smaller than their accepted ancestors, and their skulls had diminished in size and become more refined; also, according to Schwidetsky, the 'Mechta-Afalou' types had even developed prominent cheekbones. Compared to such differences, the first islanders and their descendants amongst the present people seem indistinguishable. Roughly speaking then, the immigration is most likely to have occurred *late on* in the period 3000 BC–AD 1400, and this fits in with the Mauretanian exiles theory.

The relevant physical evolution of the 'Early Mediterraneans' began once they had established their numerical domination of North Africa—which has lasted to the present—following their displacement of the 'Mechta-Afalous' by about 3000 BC. The evolution of the latter physique probably took place in refuge zones such as the Atlas mountains: the *primitive* 'Mechta-Afalou' skeleton has not been found nearer to the Canaries than the Dar es Soltan cave north of Casablanca, 1,000km from the nearest crossing point to Fuerteventura, and retreating to the mountains is more in keeping with the unenterprising 'Oranian' hunters than, say, the making of boats to navigate to islands of which they were unlikely to have had knowledge. In Roman North Africa, some 3,000 years later, a round-up of dissident hinterland tribesmen could thus include *well-evolved* 'Early Mediterraneans' and 'Mechta-Afalous': the first Canary Islanders, perhaps.

Here it should be added that, if the first islanders crossed to the Canaries from the *adjacent* part of Africa—no matter when —then that region, Spanish Sahara, should hold skeletons and relics of an everyday life both much like theirs. However, few archaeologists have visited Spanish Sahara—under strict military control, it is a desert the size of Great Britain—and reports are hard to come by. Almagro Basch summarised the position there in 1946. Some hundred pre-Islamic sites had been located, two-thirds of these Neolithic-of-Capsian-tradition, the rest Palaeolithic. No excavating had been done, consequently no skeletal material was available; however, quantities of finely worked Neolithic-of-Capsian-tradition flints had been collected off the midden surfaces, and also a fair amount of potsherds and decorated fragments of ostrich-eggs. The unspecialised Canary stone tools bear no resemblance whatsoever to the Saharan implements, although the Tenerife Guanches used high-grade obsidian and thus could have made any tools of which they had knowledge. A dozen of the Neolithic sites are clustered around Cape

47

Juby, from which Fuerteventura is visible: pottery decoration there was quite unlike that on any of thousands of sherds examined by the author on Fuerteventura. Almagro Basch reasonably suggests that in the Spanish Sahara, where no trace of Mediterranean civilisation has ever been found, Neolithic-of-Capsian-tradition culture probably long survived the appearance of the Phoenicians in the far north. The importance of this in settling the origins of the conquest time Canary islanders is of course that, if the latter came from the Spanish Sahara region, they clearly did not do so until its Neolithic-of-Capsian-tradition culture had disappeared. But even then, where, say generally south of the Atlas, are the traces of the culture from which the islanders stemmed? On the other hand there *are* cultural links with the zone of Roman activity, as will be seen shortly.

The traditional great stature of the pre-conquest men has always raised much admiration; those surprised by the anthropologists' recent conclusion that the average prehistoric islander was only of *medium* height may be interested in the details. Remains of almost 2,000 individuals were measured; however, the museums had so muddled the bones that the results are simply overall averages. Gran Canaria, with a majority of long, narrow faces of 'Early Mediterranean' descent, gave an average stature of 166·8cm for men and 153·2cm for women. Tenerife, with a majority of broad primitively robust faces of 'Mechta-Afalou' ancestry, gave 164·2cm for men and 151·9cm for women. As Hooton's measurements in fact showed fifty years ago, the men of these two islands were of medium height. Even the Fuerteventura Mahohs, just in the majority of 'Early Mediterranean' descent facially, fell below expectations—though only fifty long bones were available for measurement—the men averaging about 171·7cm, the women about 159cm. Further, the ancient Canary Islanders of 'Mechta-Afalou' ancestry—often less satisfactorily called the 'Guanche' or 'Cro-Magnon' type—have traditionally been in vivid contrast to the other group: the first were said to be very tall, much taller than the second, of light complexion and hair and blue-eyed, against the dark colouring of the shorter

48

men. But not only are the men of both groups now placed in the modern 'medium' category—except in Fuerteventura, just 'tall', but far from 'very tall'—the second group is actually rather the taller. However, it is true that the women of both groups were 'tall', though here again the second group is taller than the first. Further, whilst blond and blue-eyed individuals did occur, the evidence of the mummies is that their occurrence has probably been exaggerated. One is led to reconsider the individual descriptions of the islands by the conquest chroniclers : of Fuerteventura, 'very brave and of great stature' and again later, 'of great stature, both men and women'; of Hierro, Lanzarote and La Palma, 'a very fine people'; of Gran Canaria, Tenerife and Gomera, 'very tall people'. There is also a mention of a Fuerteventura *'géant de neuf pieds de long'* whom the French killed in combat. Perhaps attention should now be paid to the height and colouring of the *conquerors*, for they would measure the islanders against themselves. Soon after the conquest there are more descriptions, legendary, perhaps with no more than a grain of freakish truth : Galindo said that on Fuerteventura there was a tomb of the giant Mahan, 22ft tall, Espinosa reported a Gran Canaria man 14ft tall. When giants had to be found for Tristan and Isolde in 1534, the Sevillian author decided upon Fuerteventura; and his city had by then seen many Canary slaves. A no doubt equally unscientific note comes from the present Canary shepherds when, from time to time, they rout a skeleton out of its resting-cave : 'they were big men all right', they always say. Some of the past scientific anthropological work on the islanders also need to be refocused against unambiguous standards. About 1930, Fischer analysed the descriptions contained in the seventeenth-century Archivo de Indias of the Canary Islanders who were then emigrating to South America; the proportion of tall people and pale skins was, he said, clearly higher than on the Spanish peninsula at the time of his study. Torres Campos, writing in 1901, said that the Fuerteventura men were then the tallest Spaniards. Another analysis by Fischer, this time of the local people amongst a group of twentieth-century Canaries soldiers, produced the same result as his first. However, according to Hooton's tables, the average Spanish male is only 162cm in height; and the Spaniards are not, on average, a light-skinned nation. There seem to be grounds for somewhat reshaping the traditional picture of the primitive islander.

To finish with the physical types, here are the results of Schwidetsky's recent field study of the evolved 'Mechta-Afalous' amongst the *present* Tenerife people : the ancient stock was numerically strongest amongst the mountain-dwellers, the most isolated group, and the next highest, as one might expect, was the poorest class in general. The plates on pages 90, 108, and 143–4 illustrate two 'Mechta-Afalou' faces, a fisherman and a woman potter, and two 'Early Mediterranean' ones, both 'half-profits' workers; all four are from remote regions of the island. So much for the evidence of the physiques.

Many other points about the pre-conquest islanders are in accordance with an early first millennium Mauretanian origin, though this does not mean that they prove it of themselves. Both the blood of the ancient islanders and that of the present people of the Atlas are concentrated in the O group; however, this is common in long-isolated areas, so all one can say is that the results of the blood analyses do nothing to disprove Mauretanian origin for the islanders. The people of La Palma called their island 'Benehoare' and Glas reasonably compared this with the Beni-Howare tribe in the Middle Atlas of Morocco; again, the island of Gomera and the present Ghomera tribe of the Rif, also Morocco; and, in support of the conquest-time observations, one can point out that the present Riffian people have a strikingly blond element amongst them. Bride-fattening still occurs amongst the NW Saharan Tuat. Tumulus burials in some islands are comparable to those of pre-Islamic NW Africa. By the time of Christ only a very limited number of metal tools and weapons were in use in Mauretania; deportation would be an additional reason for the total lack of such finds and of other objects of mainland manufacture, since little of value, certainly not metal arms, could be taken. Then there is the amphora, dated to the late Roman period, recently found off Graciosa; it may just be connected. Also explained would be the carving of pot-lids out of travertine in Fuerteventura and the unusual burrowing-out of underground dwellings in one or two islands—not into mountain faces, like caves, but into the ground—since identical travertine covers the plain around Marrakesch, and even now the people there dig chambers into it. Then there is the recorded belief of the Tenerife Guanches that they were descended from sixty original settlers, for to take a shipload of exiles to each island smacks of Roman colonial forethought and orderliness. And, exiled from the Mauretanian interior, this would also explain the utter lack of ships and seamanship, and thus of inter-island and exterior communication, at the time of the conquest.

For it is a startling fact that the early Europeans reported the absence of a knowledge of the art of navigation and an almost total absence of any sort of craft; the exception was a mention, by Gadifer's priests, of some Gran Canaria islanders who went out to the conquerors' ship in a *'bastel'* to barter. Not that, even now, there is a shortage of wood in five of the islands, they still have forests. That the first Europeans were not deceived is suggested by the following Hierro legend : the islanders' thirteenth century prophet Yone announced that, after his death, the god Eraoranhan would come to them across the sea in a white house, and they were to receive him well, since he only came to be good to them, a welcome of which slave-hunters no doubt took ruthless advantage. Perhaps it was that in the Bimbachos' tongue their own vessels were rendered as 'white houses', but—since that is how a sailing ship would appear at a distance to a people who probably lived in shacks of brown lava—it is more probable that they just had no word for boat, having long forgotten it, and no longer in fact had a knowledge of navigation.

However, a second reference to boats does exist, though the work which contains it was not written until 1590 : the Italian architect Torriani said, in discussing another aspect of the islanders, that a few Gran Canaria people used to go across to Fuerteventura aboard 'little constructions made of dragon or palm'. Now the historian Serra Rafols has recently drawn attention to a mention in the 1506 MS of the Portuguese Valentim Fernandes of a similar-sounding craft then in use by the inhabitants of the Bahia del Galgo, somewhat to the south of the Canaries, and now the site of Port Etienne. They fish, wrote Valentim Fernandes, from a raft made of corded tree trunks, propelling it not by sail but by pieces of wood used oarwise at the back, the water halfway up their legs. To this suggestion one can add a further note : a detailed description by Robin of the early twentieth-century fishing methods of the Port Etienne Imraguens, who have had the monopoly of inshore fishing along that coast 'since time immemorial', makes no mention of boats whatsoever—although fair-sized nets are used and have to be dragged through the shallows. The Imraguen, who in fact occupy the coast as far north as Fuerteventura, seem to be of Arab rather than of pre-Islamic origin, but they may have had predecessors with a similar way of life. Perhaps the Canary Islanders were of the pre-Imraguen people—and forgot their ancient rafts in the same way as, in the four hundred years, the Imraguen appear to have done. And, after reading Valentim Fernandes' description, nothing could be more natural! Still, fifty sea-miles—and four times as far to the distant islands—is a long way if the water is up to the voyager's knees and he has only a rough piece of wood with which to propel his heavy raft, and one cannot see such craft encouraging the pioneering spirit, which had to take precious animals and grain aboard too.

Out of all the more probable pictures of the arrival of the first main immigration, the most acceptable seems that of rebellious Mauretanian tribesmen being put ashore, with some cereal seed and livestock, from large and relatively safe Roman-commanded ships. Many islands have no doubt been first populated by political exiles and convicts. The galleys disappeared, and the immigrants started to adapt themselves. Dwellings, querns, pots, tools, were needed. Though their physiques were of the oldest Mauretanian stock, they were probably from several different

Page 53: (left) Mimus or tree tobacco, a nineteenth-century arrival from South America and (above) sea-spurge, a euphorbia, both in the Jandía Jable; (below) Cactus-like *cardones*, also euphorbias, below Monte Cardón

Page 54: (right) *Mahoh* shouldered ostrich-egg pot with carved travertine lid, held by Betancuria museum's keeper; *(below)* El Saladillo. Mahoh lava-field cells. Figure stands in common courtyard

tribes, and there would have been as many dialects amongst them as there would be nowadays, though some or all may have had a common distant origin and still held common elements.

LANGUAGE

The pre-conquest speech, even as it is now known, contains much of interest. First, the few island inscriptions. Not very helpful are some non-alphabetic ones, including a few spirals which are often compared to those of the northern Megalith-builders. In North Africa, spiral cults could have lasted a long time, even up to the seventh century AD Arab invasion, particularly in a cultural backwater such as the Atlas mountains. It is probable that in the interior at least, religious beliefs, perhaps slow to reach there, took long to die. It does not seem far-fetched to suppose that, in Mauretania about the time of Christ, there would be at least remnants of the limited earlier incursions of more advanced Mediterranean cultures. This would explain not merely the spirals but also the Canaries' few 'violin-shaped' idols. Or the spirals, very limited in number, may have been the work of the few people who appeared and disappeared before the time of Juba II. Or, associated with all manner of squiggles, they may be a product of local imagination. Anyway, there seems to be nothing truly Megalithic about the pre-conquest ruins. The islanders did often use large stones, but then they accepted all those that were nearby, lumps of any size; on the other hand, the Mediterranean Megalithic constructions, for example the hundreds on the island of Menorca, are made of large shaped blocks of regular size which, it seems, were a part of the regular technique. As to general shape, the Galdar necropolis of Gran Canaria is considered to be the archipelago's most Megalithic architecture : it gave a carbon dating of the eleventh or twelfth century AD. On Fuerteventura, the unique Jandía wall is often cited as evidence of Megalithic culture; as the reader will later see, it is just a simple narrow-width wall, and it is anyway fantastic to propose that the islanders' sole manifestation of a Mega-

D

lithic background would be to make a five-kilometre wall across an isthmus, probably the last construction of which an immigrant African people, from the mountains or not, could have had experience. No, too much should not be made of the Canaries' few spirals; and, even if they are of Megalithic origin, they could have been cut quite late.

There is no reason to suppose that the conquest-time islanders made inscriptions of any sort, nor had a knowledge of writing. But, nevertheless, a few alphabetic inscriptions have been found, mainly in remote Hierro, significantly perhaps. Although undeciphered, they are said to be definitely comparable to the Tifinagh inscriptions of the central Sahara. Still being produced, by Berber speakers, the earliest of these Saharan inscriptions depict scenes of North African life between, it is thought, AD 300 and 400. These include men who, in addition to carrying round shields and javelins, are wearing headgear with feathers stuck in it; the *guapil* of the pre-conquest Lanzarote men was a skin bonnet with three feathers in it, and there are reports that the primitive Canary Islanders made shields out of roundels of dragon trunk and used wooden spears of various length.

The most important live-language notes are those of the Europeans who, from the fourteenth century, broke the islanders' isolation : one way or another, there have been recorded two long sad songs, a couple of dozen phrases, like *'Zahanat guayohec'*, or 'I am your vassal', two hundred common words and four thousand place-names. Even if care was taken to get them down as they sounded, and at first hand—neither at all certain— the words had still to be interpreted into the spelling of the Europeans' own current pronunciation of their particular languages. Recco, whose expedition will be described later, was a Genoan and for him most of the numbers from one to ten apparently sounded as in Italian : *nait, smetti, amelotti, acodetti, simusetti, sesetti, satti, tamatti, aldamorana, marava.* Sosa, who took his from the now lost account by Cedeño, who seems to have been in the islands in 1477, gives *ben, lini, amiat, arba, cansa, sumus, sat, set, acot, marago*; if these are 1477 speech, no matter whether in conquered or unconquered islands, the list is bound to be much less pure than Recco's, almost a century and a half earlier. One notes that some are much the same on each list, others totally different. Possibly these lists are from different islands, since the chroniclers of the *conquistadores* recorded that they were of *'divers loys et de divers lengages'*, which is to be expected if, starting from somewhat dissimilar laws and dialects, they had been separated for a thousand years. Possibly some at least of the two hundred recorded words are too corrupted for their origins ever to be traceable. Many sound rather too Castilian. But, where lists from the different islands were made and preserved, they do show a fair number of common words : *guánigo*, which was a type of pot and recorded in all but La Palma, and a word still in use; a smock or tunic made from skins or palm frond, with a possible parallel still worn on the continent, was called a *tamarco* in the three eastern islands; *aho*, milk, in Fuerteventura, Lanzarote and Tenerife; *banot*, a fighting staff, in Hierro, Gomera and Tenerife. Finally, the place names : like many words of pre-conquest origin, they began with *'ch-'* or *'t-'*, the latter sometimes at least simply a spelling corruption of the former, or began or ended with *'gua-'*; such names still occur plentifully in every island. In Fuerteventura, remote Chilegua is probably a good example.

Here again only a brief summary of the possible origins of these few words, no doubt a travesty of the speech of the pre-conquest people, can be attempted. Several dozen have a strong similarity to words in present Berber dialects. Glas made a fair number of close and convincing comparisons. The names of two tribes have been given already. A further example : of the many tribes still partly or entirely Berber-speaking, the Shluh group live in the Moroccan Atlas, and their word for 'barley' is *tumzzen*—as in Glas' day—whilst the Fuerteventura Mahohs are recorded as calling that important grain *tamocen*. But there are many pre-conquest words which are *not* current Berber, nor have they been located in any other known tongue, and it has recently been suggested, against some opposition, that the islanders spoke a language in its own right, and not merely a Berber dialect; like Berber and Egyptian, it would be of Hamitic origin, and have long ago travelled westwards from beyond the eastern end of the Mediterranean. Not conflicting with this, an interesting speculation is whether the unknown words in the islanders' tongues may not be remnants of the Oranian speech—which would have survived in the Atlas mountains with the 'Mechta-Afalou' physique. Equally, the words which also coincide with present Berber would have come from the speech of the early first-millennium Mauretanian descendants of the Capsian 'Early Mediterraneans'. In other words, the prehistoric Canary tongue may have those of the Oranians and Capsians in its ancestral line.

ARTEFACTS

Still unconsidered are a number of material objects which go with the ancient islanders' skeletons—and other prehistoric African objects, equally significant, not found on the islands. First, the querns. Agriculturalists usually grind their grain, even if they don't make bread. Since rotary querns have been found in *all* the islands, by the time of the conquest agriculture was known throughout the archipelago, though perhaps it had only come to be practised intensively on the heavily-populated islands. But the rotary quern was only *invented* just before the time of Christ, and then only in the Middle East, and the knowledge of it would have taken time to reach NW Africa: the rotary quern at least could not therefore have reached the islands until the time of Christ. Some few *dish*-querns have been found, mainly in Gran Canaria and Hierro; this type of quern dates back to the world's earliest agriculture. It is unlikely that Gran Canaria and Hierro were inhabited whilst Tenerife was not, nor is it likely that agriculture was long practised on Gran Canaria and Hierro but not on an inhabited Tenerife. The rotary quern is still in use in the Atlas; but some African tribes, like the Kikuyu, still grind grain in dish-querns, and a few of the early Canary immigrants may have been conservative too. But another use the primitive querns have often had—for which the rotary quern is unsuitable —is as a mortar for pounding up colours, earth for pottery-making, and roots; in Hierro, where some of the few dish-querns have been found, the Bimbachos commonly made root-flour. The archipelago could have been first inhabited by a wave of pastoralists without a knowledge of agriculture, but, lacking any dependable evidence of this or of two groups of arrivals with an important time interval between them, it seems most scientific to tend towards the obvious : that a post-Juba immigration brought with it agriculture and the rotary quern and populated then uninhabited islands.

Once again supporting a late dating is the archipelago's utter lack of Neolithic-of-Capsian-tradition flint-work, already discussed in the paragraph on the prehistory of Spanish Sahara. In the Atlas too the techniques would have long remained current, until, well after 1000 BC, the degenerating stone tools came to co-exist with the gradually increasing metal implements; however, especially away from the north coast, metal would have been so slow in coming into common use that stone—gradually losing the techniques of the Neolithic-of-Capsian-tradition—probably continued as the basic tool-material until quite recently. It was only about the time of Christ that workable iron techniques were even known in NW Africa, let alone widely enough used to challenge the stone industries. But in the Canaries there is no iron source which would have been exploitable by any smelters amongst the first arrivals, and the immigrants would have found themselves limited to the same stone implements as they had been using in their North African homeland; one can suppose these were the decadent successors of Neolithic-of-Capsian-tradition tools. Such implements could well have been the crude stone cutters and scrapers, with a few heavy types like adzes, which are found in the islands. Had an important immigration really occurred between 3000–1500 BC, as is usually maintained, it would surely have brought the specialised stone-working techniques then current in NW Africa, or at least a vestige of them. A total of four polished jadeite axes, with their origin in the European Alps, have been found in the seven islands : obviously not representative of the stone industry of the pre-conquest islanders, nor even African, they must be treated with caution. The primitive islanders' stone industry is just what one would expect of an early iron age people.

Another Neolithic craft which the Mahohs and the rest did not practise was that of spinning and weaving, already known in North Africa by 4500 BC, at Fayum in Egypt for example. No significant conclusion seems possible at present. Some prehistoric North African people are thought to have preferred leather to woven cloth, and the skin coverings of the islanders were not unsuited to the hot climate and the rough living; and, after the conquest, skin cloaks were used into the sixteenth century. Moreover, the early island goats were short-haired. Goat hair is anyway hard to work, and, perhaps, as at present in the islands, where the goats' hair is still short, it was not thought worth spinning and weaving up. The islanders probably did have sheep, but perhaps not many. No doubt their sheep's descendants have since been crossed with those caught during the fifteenth-century raids on Africa, and perhaps with others from Spain. Nowadays the animals have short thick fleeces yielding two kilos of dirty suinty wool, probably only one after washing, on analogy with Balearic sheep. The modern shepherds breed them for their fleeces—and sell the wool—and also because a mixture of sheep and goat milk gives, they say, the best cheese. Almost two thousand years ago the breed may not, perhaps, have had much wool, and may originally have been kept for skins, meat and milk, like the goats. Anyway, no spindles or looms have been found.

CONTACTS WITH THE CONTINENT

Suggestions have now been made as to the origins and date of immigration of the ancestors of the conquered islanders, as to their physique, speech and culture, as to their transport to the islands and reason for going there. Assuming them to have arrived, then, soon after the time of Christ, there was perhaps no large-scale contact with the continent for several hundred years, perhaps for as long as a thousand.

The Arabs under 'Okba invaded Morocco about AD 680. Some time between then and the extinction of the islanders as a people at the end of the Middle Ages, there were relations with the continent. In the 1477 list of numerals given above, *arba* and perhaps one or two others seem Arabic; also recorded were *almogaren*, temple, and *agadir*, granary-tower, both Arabic words. The geometrical patterns on the metal-shape pottery suggest an Islamic origin. The many clay dies are similar to those used by the Moroccans to seal their *agadir* storehouses.

However, the seals are found only on Gran Canaria, the metal-shaped, red-painted pottery almost entirely on that island, the words *agadir* and *almogaren* are given by Galindo as from Gran Canaria too. Probably only Gran Canaria is represented by the 1477 list of numerals; widespread adoption of two or three *numbers* from another tongue seems anyway unlikely, and one is forced to wonder just how representative of pre-conquest speech any of the records really are. At the most, the Arab cultural traits point to trading relations, in the main with Gran Canaria. *Agadir* is just the sort of word to be implanted in an island by Moroccan traders, and anyway, perhaps from Mauretania themselves, the islanders may have had granary-towers already, like the Fuerteventura *taro*. As for the clay seals, the traders would have established meeting places on the coast, stores would have been needed by the islanders, the Moroccans would have introduced the idea of sealing them. The speech of the islanders would soon have included the foreigners' key words. An agent or two may even have settled in Gran Canaria. *Almogaren*, temple, suggests some proselytising on behalf of Islam, though *acoran*, one of the words for 'god' in both Gran Canaria and Tenerife, was perhaps a coincidence; there is nothing peculiar to Mohammedanism in the practical forms of worship. The geometrically-patterned pottery, which Zeuner considered could be of late date, was probably the result of the trading: perhaps first acquired by the upper class of Gran Canaria and then, like the willow-pattern in modern

61

England, spreading to all the people, it probably had no religious significance in the island. Relations with the Moors did not result in the use of glazes, nor were iron tools ever apparently imported —although by AD 700 iron-working was fairly widespread in North Africa, ores being available in Morocco and the Western Sahara.

Generally, an important late immigration seems unlikely. A wave of Africans of pre-Islamic ancestry fresh from their documented resistance against the 'Okba Arabs of AD 680, or against the eleventh-century Bedouin invaders, would at least have brought metal weapons and these would then occasionally be found. The traces of Arab culture should not be over-estimated. The little coastal groups of somewhat Arabised islanders are just those likely to come forward to meet the early European navigator-chroniclers—as the modern traveller is met now by islanders with smatterings of European culture—and great use would have been made of the only few words which the two parties could have had in common, that is to say Arabic ones. Even the trading may have been quite late : the passage in which the conscientious mid-fourteenth-century Arab historian Ibn Khaldun describes four abducted islanders who were sold in Algiers suggests both that the islanders did not speak Arabic and that the Canaries were not then well known in North Africa.

And a point can be recalled to oppose the suggestion that there was a second, comparatively late, important immigration : the more and later immigrations one proposes, the more separate groups of people—each one with the vessels, skill and daring needed to cross—one has to suppose capable of utterly abandoning ship-building and navigation by AD 1341 at the latest.

REMAINING ASPECTS

The remaining aspects of Canary prehistory are either less informative or ambiguous. Of features like the mummification little of use can be said; excavations in NW Africa may yet yield parallels. Not much comparative work on the pre-conquest religious beliefs seems to have been done; Christianity, official in Roman Africa from AD 313, the time of Constantine, unofficial before, and its successor, Mohammedanism, both appear possibilities, with traces of the indigenous African animism, perhaps adapted to the current main religion, and not forgetting the spirals and 'violin-shaped' idols. Many of the more debatable material items are usually of very limited occurrence and seem best treated with caution. There is little doubt that for several thousand years before the conquest boats had been making casual landfalls on the islands, and lost and discarded equipment is only to be expected, and inscriptions too. Juba II's men noted that there had been people on the islands before them, but these were probably few and had apparently gone again or become extinct; it is just possible, but unlikely, that their organic relics will one day reach the radiocarbon laboratories.

CONCLUSION

Unless excavations yield more finely drawn details than in the past, only the mass characteristics will ever be safe ground on which to reconstruct the ancestry of the conquest-time people. Those characteristics agree well enough with the report of Juba II's expeditionaries, and also with Glas' obviously less reliable quotation about Roman Mauretanian exiles; and these, taken with the earliest of the twelve carbon dates, put the first important immigrations between AD 42 and AD 290±60, say during the first centuries after Christ.

4   THE CONQUEST

I T was the thirteenth-century advances in compass and rudder, and also the consequent improvement in maps, which led to the annihilation of the ancient inhabitants of the Canaries. The islands were probably known to classical writers, at least to Pliny, but, as Glas wrote, the often-quoted accounts of the islands 'are so indistinct and confused, that one is at a loss to know which of them they describe'; but he says the ancients obviously knew them all, including the Madeira and Cape Verd groups, but 'confounded them together under the common name of the Fortunate Islands'. To this much-discussed subject need only be added a new and concrete detail : within the last few years an amphora probably of late Roman origin has been found off Graciosa, the islet to the north of Lanzarote.

EUROPEAN PIRATES, 1291–1402

For about a thousand years after Pliny, history is silent, until, in 1291, the Vivaldi brothers lost themselves in an attempt to sail down the African coast and round to 'East India'. Rescuers and others, including a Lancelotto Malocello, followed them. Some time between 1300 and 1339 Lancelotto established himself on the Canary island now called Lanzarote after him : the first known map of the islands, a 'planisphere' by Angelino Dulcert, made in Mallorca in 1339, shows the Genoan arms upon the island of 'Lanzarotus Marocelus'. 'La Forte Ventura' is there, unclaimed apparently, and 'Vegi Marini', now translated to Isla Lobos. The eventual conquerors of the Canaries, arriving in the early fifteenth century, found Lancelotto's old fortress on Lanzarote.

The first of the many expeditions which followed the production of the planisphere was that which, in 1341, was chronicled by its second-in-command, Niccoloso da Recco. Somehow Boccaccio came to be the preserver of the account, which was only published in 1827. The ship and funds were Portuguese, the leaders Florentine and Genoan, the crew Florentines, Genoans, Castilians and other Spaniards. Relations with the islanders were typical of those of the many vessels which were to make landings on the islands in the next half-century: the Europeans seized everything they could, men, animals, everything they wanted, and then went away. Of the island which historians believe to have been Fuerteventura, Recco said: '. . . a circumference of 140 sea-miles. Just a mass of stone, uncultivated, but abundant in goats and other animals, and very much populated by naked men and women like savages'. It was from this island that they took most of their loot of goat-skins and animal fats, though they didn't dare venture inland.

Hearing about the success of the expedition, the nobility of Europe at once began to squabble for the 'legal' possession of the islands, a squabbling which lasted a century and a half. The earliest 'grant' of the Canaries, made in 1344 by the Avignon pope, Clement VI, to the Infanta Luis de la Cerda, led to no practical action in the islands. Only the British were not interested in the Fortunate Isles: so unaware of them were they that, according to Glas, upon hearing of the grant to the Infanta, the English embassy in Rome 'immediately dispatched an express to their court, to prevent this conveyance, imagining there were no other Fortunate Islands than those of Great Britain'.

However, the news had spread to all classes of Mediterraneans, and the square-sailed *coques* of the rich and practical Mallorcan merchants soon began to appear in the Canaries, where they made many raids during the second half of the century. When, in 1402, the conquerors in turn arrived, they noted that Lanzarote 'used to be heavily populated but the Spaniards and Aragonese and pirates have caught so many of the people. . . .'

Ibn Khaldun, writing in the second half of the fourteenth

century, confirms this, saying that the 'Francos', probably the Mallorcans, sold a number of the islanders in Morocco. The Sultan acquired them and, once they had learnt the language, they described their customs, saying that they kept goats and grew barley, used horns to dig and throwing stones to fight, and prostrated themselves before the rising sun.

The church was not to be left out. In 1352 a Bishop Bernat, charged with founding a Seat, Cathedral and City in Gran Canaria, equipped himself with interpreters from amongst the islanders in slavery in Mallorca. Nobody knows whether he ever set off, but in 1394 the incumbent of the Bishopric was a Dominican living in Mallorca. The already suffering islanders probably did not feel the strength of all-justifying religious zeal until the next century.

It was in 1402 that the prototype of Cortes and Pizarro, a French adventurer called Gadifer de la Salle, set his ship towards the Canaries. The initial step in the present five- or six-hundred-year period of general European colonialism had been taken— the Canaries were the first land to be annexed by the north. As will be seen, the ostensible aim was to sow Christianity, the real goal was to harvest slaves, goats and orchil. Briefly, the conquest of the islands, begun by Frenchmen in 1402, was sold soon after to the Spanish and finished by these by 1496. The first phase, the French incursions into Fuerteventura and two other of the four weaker islands, between 1402 and 1405, was chronicled by the expedition priests. However, two manuscripts exist : the more reliable, which runs up to 1404, and another, covering the whole period, which is a much later and quite obvious falsification in favour of the man who cunningly deprived Gadifer of his share of the conquest, Jean de Bethencourt. The present book is based all but entirely on the very detailed earlier MS, only events after 1404 and a few minor points, such as a landscape feature, being taken from the clumsy re-writings of Bethencourt's apologist. The second phase of the conquest, the Spanish attacks on the large islands between 1483 and 1496, is clearly enough documented. Thanks to the naïveté of the various fifteenth-century chroniclers,

66

it is clear that the islanders, defending their lives and land, were almost always trusting and humane. And that the invaders were a merciless, greed-motivated rabble of adventurers. Like any conquest, it was a succession of diverse forms of human evil and suffering. Upon this foundation is built the history of the Canaries.

GADIFER'S VOYAGE AND FIRST LANDING

Gadifer de la Salle is described by his chroniclers, the priests Bontier and Le Verrier, as a *'Poytevin du pais de Touarsoys'*, or from the region of the present Thouars in the ancient province of Poitou—just inland from the west coast of central France, near the present Poitiers. On 1 May 1402, in his own boat and with 280 men, he set sail from the nearby port of La Rochelle. He seems from the start to have been a poor judge of character, a weakness which got him into trouble time and again, and cost him not merely his men and his materials, and almost his life, but even his place in history. For to him, for his leadership and daring in the reconnaissances, for his determination to survive and go on with the conquest in the midst of treachery and abso-lute lack of supplies and support, for his merciless extermination of the islanders once his mutinous henchmen had made peaceful means impossible—for all this, to Gadifer if to anyone must go the doubtful honour of the title of conqueror of the Canaries.

At the Cantabric port of La Coruña the men mutinied. At the next port, Vivero, Gadifer's partner, Jean de Bethencourt, got them involved in an unsavoury incident, but Gadifer pulled up his anchor and left. Reaching Cádiz, they went up to Seville for supplies, only to be imprisoned for a while as pirates. There too there was a mutiny, followed by the desertion of three-quarters of the crew. They reached Lanzarote, with only 63 men, in July 1402, and anchored in the strait between Graciosa and the main island, and Gadifer then made a reconnaissance of the interior. Next they sailed round to the southern end of Lan-zarote where, after making a peace treaty with the islanders, they built a fortress on the shore of the strait between Lanzarote and Fuerteventura.

About September 1402, the Frenchmen crossed the 12km strait to prospect Fuerteventura. Leaving Bethencourt aboard the ship, off what is now Corralejo, 'Gadifer and Remonnet de Levedan with some of their companions set off at night into the island, as far as they could, until they reached a mountain where there is a running spring, six leagues from Isla Lobos'. At this time of year the arid north would have been very lightly populated. 'And they put much trouble into looking for people; but everybody had retreated to the other end of the land, as soon as they had seen the ship come into the anchorage'. Some 27km into the north, and having perhaps missed the small Mahoh settlement at Villaverde, the Frenchmen would have reached one of the map's few springs: Fuente de Hijas. 'And Gadifer and his companions stayed there eight days, until lack of bread forced them back to the port of Lobos.' And then back to the boat, apparently without so much as a slave or a goat to show for the expedition.

Meanwhile a third mutiny had taken place on board, and this although Bethencourt had stayed on the boat. The rebels only allowed Gadifer and his party back aboard on condition that they could take the ship and go home. So, with Bethencourt aboard—he was to get food and reinforcements—they went back to Europe soon after, leaving Gadifer and his dwindling group at the Lanzarote fortress. It was then September 1402 and, although Bethencourt was to send supplies by Christmas, it was not in fact to be until 1st July 1403 that he got anything to them.

GADIFER'S SECOND LANDING

About the beginning of October 1402, after Bethencourt and the mutineers had left for Europe, La Salle made his second crossing to Fuerteventura, this time landing on Lobos. Armed with long-bows and cross-bows, he came to hunt seals, *loups marins*, or *lobos marinos* in old Castilian, hence the islet's present name.

68

These animals used to live on its shores in great number—'their skins and fats would yield 500 ducats annually', noted the chronicler-missionaries. Gadifer's immediate need, they wrote, was for skins with which to make shoes for his fellow-conquerors since 'for lack of these there was not one of them who could go anywhere or do anything'. Why they couldn't make them from goat-skin is not explained, and it is possible that seal-catching for profit was the real aim. The chroniclers do not say whether they caught any seals.

Lobos is triangular in shape, the longest coast, facing east, no more than three kilometres in length, the others a little shorter, and La Salle could have explored the whole island in an hour or two. The dominant feature is the 122m red cone which forms the corner of the two shorter sides, falling straight into the breakers at the point nearest the main island. Just in from the east coast there is a marshy salt-water lagoon, but the islet has no fresh water. After a few days Gadifer sent Remonnet de Levedan back in the boat to the Rubicon fortress for supplies, because Lobos was 'a desert island and without water'; he and ten others stayed behind, with two days' supply of food. However, back at the fortress, Bertin de Berneval, the acting commander, was betraying Gadifer. A Spanish slave-catching boat, the *Tajamar*, had anchored in the north of Lanzarote and the islanders had turned to their alliance with the French for protection. Berneval told them to group themselves together for safety and he would see that they were all right. Then, of course, he caught them and, presumably marching them to the northern end, handed them over to the slavers, with whom he had made an agreement. All except the King of Lanzarote, who 'daring and strong, broke his bonds and freed himself from his three guards, one of whom, a Gascon, chased him; but the King turned on him furiously and gave him such a blow that the others let him go; and this was the sixth time that he escaped from the hands of the Christians, by his courage'. For all La Salle's lack of scruples, it was obvious that, as the leader and a tactician, he would not approve of Berneval's action. So, when Gadifer's

69

men came in from Lobos for supplies, those mutineers who were at the fortress seized their boat, Beneval's henchman 'the Bastard of Blesy' driving Remmonet de Levedan away from it at sword point. About to depart, the mutineers started to destroy the stores. Soon Berneval got back overland with thirty Spaniards from the *Tajamar,* which was waiting their return in Graciosa, and, after a huge and deliberately wasteful meal, finished off the looting of the fortress, piling up both La Salle's boat and the *Tajamar's*—which had come round with seven more Spaniards in it—with the expedition supplies and arms, and wrecking all he couldn't take, ending up by pouring their last barrel of wine out onto the ground. The Spaniards, in the meantime, were raping a number of French women whom Berneval had handed over to them, and whom, since they were from Poitou, one can suppose to have been attached to La Salle's party. Remmonet de Levedan's pleas to be allowed to send food to the starving seal hunters brought a spate of abuse from Berneval, 'whom Gadifer trusted as none other'. 'I'd like him to know,' said Berneval, 'that, if he wasn't older than me, I'd kill him myself. But, as it is, if he gives any more trouble I'll have him drowned, that'll show him how to hunt seals.'

Back on Lobos, La Salle was soon out of drinking water. 'Each night he put a strip of cloth out on the ground to soak up the dew, and then squeezed it out and drank the drops.' Probably hunger was less of a problem : the seals, the birds in the marshy lagoon, the crabs and the limpets, all would have kept the band alive. Perhaps no Mahoh had ever been there, as the islanders had no boats, although they were good swimmers, and the French were not in danger. Waiting for relief from Lanzarote, they may have seen their boat and another, unknown, set off in the opposite direction, north up the Lanzarote coast : Bertin de Berneval and the Spaniards taking the loot up to the waiting *Tajamar* off Graciosa.

Luckily for Gadifer, his men were still trying to help him. They sent the expedition's two priests and two shield-bearers overland to Graciosa, a distance of 60 kilometres. Arriving before the boats,

Page 71: The Conquerors, 1402, frontispiece of Gadifer's MS. Gadifer with plume, sword and shield, Bethencourt with plume and sword only

Page 72: (above) Farmhouse of El Cortijo Antiguo. Dragon tree at centre and wind-driven water-pump with cistern on right; (below) Village church, Tisca-manita, on central plain

the quartet enlisted the sympathy of the captain of another Spanish ship, the *Morella*. The *Morella* had in fact reached there before the *Tajamar* but, on being approached by Bertin with the same offer as the one which the *Tajamar* later accepted—to take forty slaves and Bertin and clear out—the captain had refused, saying it was treachery. Now he helped Gadifer by sending a man back overland to the Rubicon, apparently with oars, and he and four of Gadifer's loyal men ventured across in a little boat which Bertin did not think worth taking. It sounds as though it was a hard crossing, but they rescued Gadifer and his men, all getting back safely to the fortress.

Bertin's boats, in the meantime, reached Graciosa. One was Gadifer's property, and both were piled high with the expedition stores and gear, including 'several crossbows and all the long-bow strings and a great quantity of thread for making crossbow cords, and all the arms, of which there were a lot, fine and good ones . . . and they even had to damage a fine cable we had . . . and, as well, the Spaniards took off four dozen arrows; and they broke into two of Gadifer's coffers and helped themselves, and took other things too many to list'. But the priests and squires were waiting for them when they arrived off Graciosa, and, taking the *Morella*'s captain with them, riskily went aboard the *Tajamar* and confronted Berneval and his gang of French mutineers and Spanish accomplices.

The absconding traitor tried to get the priests to admit that all he was carrying off was his own property. But they disagreed and, when they insisted that he had joined the expedition without anything, and even reminded him that Bethencourt had lent him a hundred francs in Paris, he tried to end the argument by saying : 'All right, I'll go straight to Spain and give Bethencourt anything that's his, and you mind your own business!' But the priests and squires went on with their claim, and Berneval eventually let them take back their boat, and even tossed one of the expedition interpreters, 'Isabel the Canary woman', in after them, literally. They fished her out before she drowned and rowed away indignantly.

However, Bertin, about to leave the scene for ever, had not yet finished. There was still the question of those who helped him in the mutiny : he got them ashore under a pretext and, with a last shout of 'Fix yourselves up as best you can, for you'll not be coming with me', Bertin disappeared northwards aboard the *Tajamar*, with the expedition gear and captured islanders. Then, of course, those left on the shore were suddenly very penitent, and went whining to the priests and squires, who were presumably about to set off back, wanting Gadifer to pardon them. They persuaded one of the squires to walk to the south at once, to find the expedition chief and ask his clemency. Once their emissary had gone, the mutinous group thought of an even better scheme, and seized the much-disputed boat, presumably from the three who remained, and set off for Africa. 'And as far as they are concerned', says the chronicler-priest, 'they went off and drowned themselves five hundred miles away and of the twelve only two escaped and these were made slaves. . . .'

And, with one thing and the other, and Bethencourt's non-appearance, Gadifer de la Salle was very much saddened and self-righteous. But he was soon working out similar plots to remedy the situation, and taking his revenge where he could. From then onwards it was open war with the Lanzarote people, who had begun 'with demonstrations of friendship, as was their custom' but were now of course enraged at the French treachery. The *conquistadores* simply spent their time killing, or catching the islanders and bartering them for badly-needed supplies with any passing ship. This lasted until the Castilian boat brought them provisions, nine months later.

GADIFER'S THIRD LANDING

In July 1403, aboard the supply ship, Gadifer made a pirate's circuit of the archipelago, in particular exploring the centre of Fuerteventura. The latter part of the narrative begins abruptly with his entry into the lower end of the Río Palmas valley. The pass is dominated by the hummocks of the Risco del Carnicero, and the pre-conquest settlement amongst them will be described in Chapter 6. The defile into the valley's lower end 'is so impregnable that a single man could hold it against all comers, for it is not two stone's-throw long and only three or four fathoms wide'. So wrote Gadifer's chroniclers. But the Mahohs, who must have watched from the well-hidden cells up on the southern side of the hummocks, made no move to defend the pass. Gadifer and his gang 'had to take off their shoes in order to cross the marble stones, which were so smooth and slippery that one has to go on all fours and, even so, those at the back had to hold out their lances for the front ones to push against, and then the front ones pulled the others after them'. This clowning was the time for the Mahohs to deal with the French as the islanders of Gran Canaria were to deal with Pedro de Vera's men eighty years later: the Spaniards were heavily defeated at the battle of Ajodar by having boulders dropped upon them in a narrow pass. But Gadifer and the Mahohs had not yet come face to face, and it was left to the invaders to attack first. And so, on the other side of the pass, they found only 'a flat and beautiful valley, a very pleasant place, where there must be some 900 shady palm, and streams of water running down the middle, and the palms are in groups of 100 to 120, the tallest like masts, more than 20 fathoms high, and so green, so thickly fronded and so heavy with dates that they are a pleasure to see'. No doubt the Mahohs grew barley in the well-watered valley, but this would have been harvested well in advance of the July heat. There, and probably overlooked from the hummocks by the wondering islanders and their families, Gadifer and his companions 'ate in the delicious shade, upon the fine green grass, near to the running streams, and rested a little, because they were very tired'. And then they set off again, up a great slope—probably the western cordillera—and Gadifer told three of the men to go on ahead. 'And as soon as the three did so they met their enemies.' This is the very first encounter, but it is noticeable that the Mahohs were already considered 'enemies'. Pietre, one of the expedition interpreters and a Gran Canaria native 'pursued three of them and took a woman from them and surprised two more in a cave, one of whom had a child at the breast, which she strangled for fear that it should cry out'. After this triumph the conquerers climbed up the western cordillera and, presumably from the heights, saw '*un mauvais pays*', certainly the Gairía lava-fields, some way away across the central plain. 'There', said Gadifer, no doubt rubbing his hands, 'there are bound to be people'. More people who could be sold into slavery.

> 'So he ordered that some of his few men should beat the whole of the badland; and they spread themselves out wide apart, as only eleven had stayed with Gadifer. It fell to the Castilians who had not deserted to come across a group of people, forty-five or fifty in number, who attacked the Castilians and kept them off until their women and children had escaped. The rest of Gadifer's men, who were spread out quite a way away, heard the shouts and came as fast as they could, and the first to arrive was Remmonet de Levedan on his own, who attacked them; but they utterly surrounded him, and if it hadn't been for Jennequin d'Auberbouc, who arrived at that moment and threw himself at them and forced them to retire, Remmonet might have been killed. Jeuffroy d'Ansonville also arrived, bow in hand, and never more needed, and between them they put them to flight. But Gadifer, who had been far ahead in the badland, and who was coming with all speed, with three more men, went straight for the mountains where they were going, and was about to cut them off, when night fell, and he got so near that he spoke to them, and only with great difficulty could our men recognise each other, as it was so dark. And it took them all night to get back to their base, without having captured more than four women.'

CONQUEST

In September 1403, a year after Bethencourt's departure, Lanzarote was declared pacified. Gadifer had been merciless. At one point in the chronicle the priests wrote that when the expedition arrived in Lanzarote the island had 'some 300 people, whom we have caught with great difficulty and much work, and by the grace of God baptised'. But, elsewhere and more grimly, they

76

estimated '200 fighting men' and, in another place, that they had killed 'more than 50' and imprisoned in the fortress 'more than 80', of whom many had died, and only baptised 80, although they said many more were giving themselves up every day. The symbolic end came in January 1404, when they finally caught the elusive king, with twelve of his subjects, and baptised him too. So much for the Lanzarote people, most of them dead or imprisoned, enslaved locally or in Europe, but all baptised. A few were probably on the run in the mountains.

Bethencourt, in Spain all this time, was alternately cheating Gadifer and being cheated himself. Somehow Gadifer's ship was sunk after arrival in Cádiz, and funds given to Bethencourt by friends of the expedition, including 20,000 maravedis from the King of Castile, went astray. The supply ship, ill-provisioned, only reached Gadifer in July 1403, in spite of Bethencourt having heard by the end of 1402 that the islanders and the French were at war. The new food soon ran out, and the capture of the island king's own store of provisions was the only further supply until Bethencourt himself did at last return, on 19 April 1404. Worn out by fighting and hunger, Gadifer's party recorded : 'And for the last two and a half years we have been sleeping on the bare ground, with no more bedding than our torn, worn-out clothes, which has been a great hardship.' During this period, actually a little under two years, Bethencourt had spent his time at the Court, getting himself the *personal* title of 'Lord of the Islands' together with the right to a *quinto*, a levy of fifth of their value on all exports—'even on those of Gadifer', wrote the chronicler in disgust in the margin. Nor did Bethencourt even bring out all the supplies given him by somebody else for the expedition. 'He kept the rest for himself', says the chronicler bitterly.

Needless to say, there was henceforth a permanent rift between Gadifer and Bethencourt. Soon after the latter's return in April 1404, they began building two more fortresses—one each, since they were now divided into two factions—in the centre of Fuerteventura, presumably taking advantage of Gadifer's reconnaissance. In no time they were passing schoolboy-like threatening notes to each other. Next they both set off to the Spanish Court, Gadifer to claim a share in the islands, Bethencourt to stop him getting it. Gadifer, not known to the king, lost, and never returned to the islands, his work there thus yielding him nothing.

Back again in Fuerteventura in October 1404, Bethencourt, by threats and strategy, took over the Gadifer party's fortress, and from then onwards one hears only of him. The extent to which Fuerteventura was really subdued by that time is uncertain; claimed as conquered in January 1405 after half-a-dozen skirmishes and without any action for which Bethencourt's personal chroniclers could praise him, the island had already been prepared by Gadifer's reconnaissances. Tenerife, Gran Canaria and La Palma held out for almost another century, Gomera was worn down by Bethencourt's successors. True, in late 1405, Bethencourt did 'conquer' Hierro : he lured the bulk of the islanders, over a hundred, to a peace meeting, and then caught and deported them all. Lanzarote was clearly Gadifer's conquest. Nevertheless, once Gadifer was out of the way, Bethencourt gave himself the title of 'King of the Canaries'.

In fact, the annexation of the Canaries only ended in 1496. For any Mahohs who remained in 1501, a ceremony took place in Fuerteventura's Castillo de Lara, a fortress said to have stood on a rocky hump a little down-valley of Betancuria. Alonso de Lugo held a symbolic 'taking possession of the island', as Adelantado or Governor of the Canaries. Whilst, a few years earlier, Columbus had been discovering America, it had been Alonso de Lugo who had been bringing the Canaries' conquest to an end by the near extermination of the Tenerife Guanches, the last of the islanders to surrender. By the end of 1494 he had strewn Tenerife with dead bodies, and plague then began to spread amongst the dispirited though unconquered Guanches. As if this were not enough, the dogs became ferociously addicted to human flesh, and the wandering islanders, many of them refugees, had often to sleep up trees for fear of attack; comparisons have been made with the rats in parts of France during the recent World Wars. Finally the Guanches became so apathetic that many simply

78

lay down in their caves and died, for lack of interest in living. Opening another series of attacks on the mountain strongholds in the summer of 1496, Alonso de Lugo found there was nothing left to fight. When asked by the Guanches why he troubled their land, he replied that it was 'to make them Christians', and, at sword point, he baptised all the survivors he could catch. Dead, shipped to the Peninsula as slaves, soon hardly a Guanche remained. In the Castillo de Lara, in 1501, Alonso de Lugo made it clear to Fuerteventura that the history of the pre-conquest Canary Islanders, as a separate people, had come to an end.

EARLY POST-CONQUEST LIFE

Having proclaimed Fuerteventura conquered in 1405, Bethencourt's script-writers concentrated on the Mahoh's great love for him. When he was going, they apparently said : 'Lord, why are you leaving us? We will never see you again. Alas ! What will happen to our country, lacking such a wise and prudent Lord, one who has put so many souls in the way of salvation'. Post-conquest society must be judged from a few notes, for example on the sharing out of Fuerteventura amongst the Norman settlers : 'It was reasonable that they should be better off than the islanders'. Had Gadifer finished the conquest instead, he would no doubt have produced a similar version in his own favour. His relatively-recently discovered 1402–4 MS has shown up the duplicity of Bethencourt's, although the latter's own inconsistency had made it suspect enough. But, of course, *after* 1404, there is only Bethencourt's, probably a distorted picture, then.

Worse still, after 1405, when in turn Bethencourt's MS ends as far as the islands are concerned, almost nothing is known of life in Fuerteventura. Historians have preferred to devote themselves to disentangling the fifteenth-century contracts of the nobility of southern Europe; during this period these gentry were endlessly selling each other the islands, usually with as much title and scruple as a gathering of horse-dealers. Whilst these manœuvres were going on, the four more or less conquered islands were being exploited by a series of local despots; of their tedious intrigues and marriages, enlivened by an occasional knife-thrust from the abused and desperate survivors of the pre-conquest people, the historians have much to say. But of the day-to-day life, almost nothing. Bethencourt's successor, his nephew Maciot, was as bad as any who ever ruled the islands, and in 1414 the Queen of Castile forcibly replaced him. Azurara noted that in 1443 the Christian population of Fuerteventura was only eighty. He probably would not have found the Mahohs willing to be counted, for, as a Madrid document dated 1647 records, about 1450 the Mahohs almost regained their island, a statement which is backed by the eye-witness narrative of Cada-mosto, dated about 1455 : the people, he wrote, are able to fortify themselves in the mountains in such a way that a serious siege is necessary to make them surrender. Bethencourt claimed to have conquered Fuerteventura by 1405, but it is far more certain that, in the middle of the century, the Mahohs were all but in control. However, the current overlord, Herrera, went to Fuerteventura and subdued them, perhaps finally. After this, information on the islanders seems once again lacking.

In order to get an idea of what life was like for the fifteenth-century Mahohs of Fuerteventura, and for the surviving islanders of Lanzarote, Hierro and Gomera, one must read the immediately post-conquest history of the three main islands, no doubt no worse than the average of conditions in Fuerteventura and the others throughout the preceding eighty years. From the capture, in 1483, of Gran Canaria, through that of La Palma in 1493 and Tenerife in 1496, the fate of the islanders is very clearly recorded. For those who were not killed in the fighting, there were, at the end of the fifteenth century, three alternatives : being deported for slavery, becoming a slave on the spot, or, finally, resisting in the mountains. These can be described one by one.

Some of the conquerors claimed that *all* the islanders were 'slaves of war'; the most reasonable held that only those taken fighting could be enslaved. The distinction was but an academic one, since the people, land and animals were in fact shared out as booty by the ruling class, Alonso de Lugo getting the true tyrant's share. Estimates of the population of Gran Canaria before its conquest in 1483 have varied between 10,000 and 60,000; by 1492 the deportations to the Peninsula had been so massive— into slavery, but partly to avoid any possibility of a revolution— that only *40 males* remained in Gran Canaria, the maximum figure specified by the Catholic Kings from Spain. Great quantities of the deported Canary Islanders lived miserably outside Seville; a steady stream of boats took them there and to Valencia between 1489–98. Some of the exiled were reduced to showing off their great agility in the streets. Most no doubt degenerated rapidly. A few got back and were again deported, others petitioned the King and were eventually allowed to return openly. By 1493 the island of La Palma had been taken over peacefully but, upon discovering what they had let themselves in for, the islanders rose and were brutally suppressed, Alonso de Lugo deporting 1,200 of them on the spot. In 1494 a cargo of humans was delivered to Ibiza, in the Balearics. In 1496 Tenerife fell and its islanders followed the rest. The Portuguese too were busy slave-catching in the Canaries, and also in the Cape Verd group, their exclusive hunting ground. The Genoese had a slave-catching boat in the Canaries by 1506, if not earlier. Transported into slavery, split up around medieval Europe— sight is lost of thousands of the ancient islanders. Soon it could be estimated that only 1,200 families remained in the *seven* islands.

History contains few more saddening spectacles than that of these deported islanders, most probably still in skins, many half-naked, all hungry, bewildered, unable to understand the language, laughed at and despised, submitted to all manner of cruelties, wandering hopelessly about the Spanish Peninsula and the Mediterranean of the Middle Ages.

The second category holds those who were enslaved on their own territory, or were shifted to another island, a move which no doubt paid. Following the end of the conquests, laws were

81

made from the Peninsula for the division of the land and water taken from the islanders : (1) plots with irrigation to be distributed in small parcels and dry land in large; (2) *conquistadores* to get more than post-fighting settlers; (3) the pre-conquest islanders 'not to be forgotten'. How reasonable, for conquerors, this sounds on paper ! Swords, or, in the islanders' case, sticks and stones, into ploughshares, and then it was to be husbandry side by side. In fact, all sorts of people were already pouring into the Canaries : planters after cheap labour, trade agents after valuable goods for next to nothing, aristocrats and parvenus, moneylenders and capitalists, all competing for a share of the loot with the *conquistadores* and immigrant Castilian *colons*. As for the ancient islanders, who were 'not to be forgotten', far from this, as slaves they were the initial labour force.

Sugar plantations, for example, the preferred investment of the capitalists, had appeared in Gran Canaria even before the fall of Tenerife. In the latter island in 1503, a document records the marriage of a *'mestre de azúcar'* with a slave woman. To work the plantations the islanders were shipped hither and thither according to supply, demand and administrative policy. In one of those poems in which, even to the present day, only the 'exotic' flavour of distant exploited lands and people is brought out, since the truth is less appealing, the sixteenth-century poet Guillaume du Bartas wrote :

> *'Pour vous, ventres goulus, pour vous il faut aller*
> *Chercher le sucre dous jusques en Canarie'*

One can hear the soft cooing of the satisfied stomachs of Europe and, as Pangloss was often to explain to Candide, all was for the best in the best of all possible worlds.

In 1498, a royal decree made all the pre-conquest people free. In the will of the Spanish governor of Gran Canaria, made in 1506, there is the following legacy : 'One old slave and one of fifteen others, both white; one old coloured slave; one white male slave in his prime; one black slave who suffers the devaluation of his race; three more female, two more male, both white and coloured'. The whites may have been captured Moors—but it is certain that in 1511 the islanders had to be decreed free a second time. And, amongst the evidence which suggests that even this decree was ignored, there is the 1513 testimony of a Spaniard well known in the islands, Guillén Castellano. He left to his wife : 'Two slaves one dark *and the other Guanche*, and a black girl'; he bequeathes twelve other slaves, giving each one a sentence of work, for his legatees, of between one and seven more years, and only then are they to be freed.

These island slaves were put, in many cases, to look after their own flocks and to farm their own land, but now, of course, for the benefit of the Europeans. Sixteen years' captivity was the legal minimum before they could be freed. The *smallest* legal punishment was a hundred lashes, man or woman. The owners themselves could whip or torture their slaves A 'freeman', or *horro*, who was maltreated and imprisoned by a gentleman, or *hidalgo*, got a hearing from the Adelantado, but was simply told that an *hidalgo* could not be punished; the Adelantado could not even rationalise the decision by pointing out that the *horro*, a Guanche in this case, had the darker skin and so was, *ipso facto*, in the wrong, for the Guanche's would probably have been at least as light as the Spaniard's. The islanders were not permitted to carry arms in the capitals. By 1506, eight years after the first decree declaring them free, the persecution was at its height. Ignoring the death penalty for escape, more and more islanders were taking to the mountains, encouraged, no doubt, by a hard and unsubmitted core which had been there since the conquest.

In 1506 the Spaniards were becoming desperate, as mounting cruelty increased the islanders in refuge : '. . . and the mountains are full of rebels and thieves, so that if nothing is done the island will be lost'. It is recorded that the refuged people formed veritable townships in the mountains, living off their goats. They were pursued as traitors and robbers; many only took away or came back to steal their own flocks; but, such must have been the mixture of despair and degradation caused by their treat-

83

ment, that many probably came down from the mountains and took anything they could. The Spaniards now formed bands from the islanders still subject to them, and, no doubt often with menaces, forced them to hunt their own kind. Any who helped the rebels were banished. In 1514 pardon was offered to those who gave themselves up within twenty days, after which they would be hunted down and hanged. To hunt them down being obviously beyond the Spaniards, and it not being clear, perhaps, why, if they were to be pardoned, they should give themselves up, the islanders stubbornly continued in the mountains : many probably objected to the suggestion that *they* had done anything wrong, for most were not born into slavery and would have had strong memories of the old free life of twenty or thirty years earlier.

The Spaniards no doubt thought it all most ungrateful. As recently as the late eighteenth century, Viera y Clavijo wrote : 'That the island people were almost wiped out by the treatment of the conquerors was without a doubt more than compensated for by the knowledge they acquired of the only true faith and of the evangelical spirit'. Some may think differently but, as Viera y Clavijo wrote of Captain Glas' adverse comments on the islands : 'such errors are inevitable in a foreigner, who sees things very superficially'.

By 1535, the Tenerife Spaniards were asking the Inquisition to come and catch the islanders, since 'the land is so broken-up and the natives, and those of the neighbouring islands, are so very sure-footed, and used to the steep faces and the rocks, where the Castilians can't go, that they have become masters of the flocks, and kill and eat more of them than the owners'.

By then, however, the focus had turned upon catching and importing Moors and Negroes for slavery in the islands. The reason is clear. Many pre-conquest women and their descendants had married the conquerors, whilst others, left with children of mixed blood, wisely declared them to be Spanish, and most, even of pure stock, gave their children Spanish names. And so enslave-able locals were soon in short supply : the *hidalgos*, as unwilling to dirty their own hands as ever, had to look to Africa. The ancient islanders gradually disappeared from the towns and plantations. At the same time, up in the mountains, the defiant rebels too seem to have gradually died out and, from the end of the sixteenth century, the high fortresses are heard of no more.

5 ENFORCED MOORISH IMMIGRATION

THE result of the disappearance of the indigenous people was a lack of slaves and, in the late fifteenth and in the sixteenth centuries, the Spaniards set about remedying the position by massive man-hunts on the adjacent African coast. Most of the captured Africans went to Lanzarote and Fuerteventura.

THE SPANISH IN AFRICA

Post-conquest life on Fuerteventura has always been linked to that on the nearby African coast, and so a summary of Spanish history in this little-known region may be of interest before coming at last to discuss the islanders' conflict and contact with the people there. The first practical Spanish interest in the coastline was the establishment, in 1476, of the fortress of Santa Cruz de Mar Pequeña by the reigning despot of the subdued islands, Diego de Herrera. This foothold, built at a place then probably called Guader, now called Puerto Cansado, and just opposite Fuerteventura, had to be relinquished half a century later. Incidentally, it was here that in 1764 Captain Glas tried to start a barter port for trade with the African people; although the place had been abandoned by them for two hundred and fifty years, the Spanish felt this an affront, and imprisoned him for a year in Tenerife. About 1500 the Spanish obtained a grip upon a separate zone a little to the north of Santa Cruz de Mar Pequeña, in the region of the present Ifni, and a few tribes were attached to Castile; but all this too was only momentary. However, between 1860 and 1912 the Spanish did acquire possession of two

86

coastal areas. One, known as Spanish Sahara, stretches up from what is now Port Etienne to a point just south of Puerto Cansado, the site of the disappeared Santa Cruz de Mar Pequeña; here the coastal boundary is with Morocco. Spanish Sahara, with a coastline 1,000km long, has an area of about a quarter of a million square kilometres and a population of some 20,000 people, mainly nomads. The other territory the Spanish obtained was Ifni, a coastal enclave within the southern end of Morocco. One estimate of Ifni's area is about 1,400sq km, just a little smaller than Fuerteventura; its population has been reckoned at some 50,000 or two and a half times that of the island. The Spanish have claimed that Ifni includes the site of Santa Cruz de Mar Pequeña—to establish a long-standing right to the Ifni zone— and Fuerteventura people who have been on the well-paid Ifni prospecting and construction work come back convinced of this; however, some Spanish historians have stood up for the facts. Ifni and Spanish Sahara, the former in a Gibraltar-like position, have long been a source of conflict between Spain and Morocco. In January 1969 Ifni was ceded to Morocco whilst, at the time of writing, Spain has also agreed—under UN Special Committee pressure—to a self-determination referendum in Spanish Sahara.

The present people of the coastal zone opposite Fuerteventura are divided into four groups. To the north, the Berber-dialect Tekna, agriculturalists and pastoralists, who have adopted Arab tents for seasonal transhumance. On a very long, narrow coastal strip, from opposite Fuerteventura down to Port Etienne, the Arabic-speaking Imraguen fishermen, sedentary. Inland of them, to the north the Regeibat, to the south the Delim, both Arabic-speakers and nomadic pastoralists.

SLAVES FROM THE AFRICAN MAINLAND

The site of Diego de Herrera's fortress and base for his raids on the continent was, then, just opposite Fuerteventura, where one would expect to find it: the present Puerto Cansado. Since AD 1300, if not before, the northern Moors had hunted the pre-conquest Canary people for slaves, though perhaps only those of the weaker islands; the Canary Europeans, however, were soon hunting the Moors, at least those on the undefended adjacent coast. Once the 1476 fortress was established, and with the aid of a renegade and knowledgeable Moor, Juan Camacho, the successive Lords of Fuerteventura and Lanzarote began a series of raids which continued until the end of the sixteenth century, and made their names the most hated in western Africa. Diego de Herrera, as incapable as Bethencourt and the rest of conquering the three main islands, carried out forty-six raids on the continent, peopling the two understandably depopulated islands with Moorish serfs. Fresh impetus was added about 1500, when the treatment of the ancient people of the recently-conquered main islands had caused them too to be in short supply : in 1505 a Royal Seal was obtained to invade Africa and catch Moors. The need became even more acute when, in 1511, the remaining native islanders were technically set free for the second time. In 1525 Charles V waived his *quinto* tax on captured Moors, by way of encouragement. For much of the sixteenth century, raiding Africa seems to have been the chief pastime of the Lord of Fuerteventura; as a twentieth-century Spanish writer puts it, this was 'for the greater glory of God and honour of Christianity'.

Captured Moors were shipped in. And, though many no doubt got back, Fuerteventura in particular became saturated with them. Then suddenly, in the second half of the sixteenth century, the situation changed. The Mar Pequeña fortress had long been lost by the Spaniards, and now well-organised Algerian and Moroccan counter-raids on the islands began . . . and the Old Christians of Fuerteventura became painfully aware that they were outnumbered by their hostile serfs. Terror spread amongst the European settlers; there are recent parallels amongst twentieth-century *colons* and colonials in many parts of Africa.

Lanzarote was attacked in 1569 by a force of 600 Moroccans in nine vessels, to be followed two years later by an assault by Algerians. In 1573 Gran Canaria was raided. Lanzarote was again attacked in 1586, by the Captain-General of the Sultan

Page 89: (above left) Cochineal on cactus *(Opuntia maxima)* near Antigua; *(above right)* State agave plantation, also near Antigua; *(below)* Drying agave fibre at La Oliva state plantation

Page 90: Tomato growing. A half-profits worker picking the crop. His 'Early Mediterranean' face contrasts with those of his family.

of Algiers at the head of seven boats bearing at least 1,000 men armed with muskets, shot-guns and crossbows; carefully planned, the aim was to catch the hated Marquis for 'offences and damages done to Barbary'. In 1593 some 600 Moors assaulted Fuerteventura and sacked Betancuria, burning down the church. By 1595 the 'Old Christians' had called a fortifications engineer to the island.

Apart from looting and wrecking, the Moors took away hundreds of islanders as slaves, whilst many of those who had been island slaves took the chance to go off with the raiders. The steady stream of relapses was not overlooked by the Inquisition, which at once confiscated any property left behind. A modern Spanish writer notes reprovingly that 'the enslaved Moors had professed themselves Christians but lightly, for material gain'.

In 1590 the trustworthy Torriani could write of the two eastern islands that 'three-quarters of the islanders are pure Moors or their children or nephews'. In 1595 Prospero Casola, the fortifications consultant, said that the Old Christians could not stand it, and had long been leaving as fast as the Moors were imported, so the total population had not in fact increased. Segregation was absolute, the Moriscos on the east, the Old Christians on the west. The centre was an area of tension; in Tiscamanita, for example, the house of one Old Christian was automatically looted by his neighbours the moment he left it. The Moriscos married only amongst themselves, and followed their own customs; the girls, for example, were often wedded at ten years old. The male serfs had to watch the flocks. The women and girls were prostituted by the Spaniards and could only avoid this by getting baptised. As had done the Mahoh women before them, many gave their children Spanish names, whether they were mixed or purely Moorish, to ensure they would not be enslaved in turn. At the end of the sixteenth century there were thirteen entirely Morisco villages in Fuerteventura. About this time the Canary Inquisitor estimated there were 307 Morisco inhabitants, more than in any other island; 1,500 was Prospero Casola's

F

estimate. The Moriscos of the Canaries were not expelled during the massive nation-wide early-seventeenth-century purge of Philip III : those who wished to stay in Spain, the free Moriscos of the Peninsula, were expelled, those who wished to go, the enslaved Moriscos of the Canaries, were kept. The King was told how the island Moriscos worked the land and generally were given all the hardest tasks . . . the Lords of Fuerteventura and Lanzarote, to whom their slaves were indispensable, made sure Philip III exempted the Canary Moriscos. Spain legally abolished slavery a century and a quarter ago.

Some have noted Negroid traces in the *pre*-conquest skeletons; recent workers deny this is so. The Negro slaves, of *post*-conquest times, were caught in Senegal and Guinea. Mainly put to work, to give pleasure to the *ventres goulus*, in the sugar plantations of the big islands, some no doubt reached Fuerteventura, as they did Lanzarote. The Cave of the Negress, at Maninubre, near Antigua, is said to be where one hid herself from pursuers; Viera y Clavijo states that, during the 1593 Moorish attack, the heiress to the lord of the island was hidden in that cave by her nurse, perhaps, then, a negress. Across the plain lies Montaña del Negrito. The late-nineteenth-century traveller Olivia Stone was told, when in Gran Canaria, of a colony of Negroes still living in the mountains there, near Tirajana; they were never seen except when they came down to work as casual hands at harvest time. The Catalan anthropologist Fusté, having studied the dermo-papillary hand lines of the present Canary people, has decided that there is no important Negro strain in them, if any at all.

The last raid by the Lord of Fuerteventura seems to have been in 1593. Internationally, the Moors had reached an apogee with their victory at the Battle of the Three Kings in 1578; from that date they declined again, and possibly a raid on Lanzarote and Gomera, in 1618, when they caught about 1,000 islanders, was their last major attack on the Canaries. Conflict did not finish entirely, however, until 1749. Henceforth contact occurred solely on the African coast. The Canary Islanders had the initiative again, but their raids were not upon the people but upon the fish.

Whereas the Canaries' coastal platforms are rough-bottomed and deep, the shallow sea-bed off the adjacent Saharan coast, level and sandy, is one of the world's best fishing grounds. As danger from the northern Moors became less, so the islanders went in increasing numbers to fish the African waters. The Canary boats there met the Imraguen, wading with their nets: relations were sometimes peaceful and barter-based, sometimes hostile. In 1765 the Spanish fishermen caught two Moorish women and they were baptised in Gran Canaria. In 1770, the Wadi Nun people cut the throats of two Fuerteventura men. In 1784 the *Angustias*, a Las Palmas fishing boat, sank off Cabo Bojador, and there was trouble saving the crew from the Moors. In the eighteenth century in Fuerteventura and other islands, many people suddenly found it desirable to claim *pre-conquest* descent, and probably anything was preferable to admitting to have Moorish blood. From first to last, the Moors have been detested in Fuerteventura, and—since now the people have blended sufficiently to be able to unite in this attitude —never more strongly than today.

MOORISH INFLUENCE

However, one way or another the Moors are responsible for many present features of the island. The low rectangular windowless dwellings which one sees everywhere are not un-African in aspect, and contrast with the spacious courtyards and the balconies and carved shutters of the more Peninsula-style farms. Both the rebuilt Betancuria church and the Antigua Ayuntamiento, the Town Hall—once perhaps the two most important public buildings in the island—have mudejar elements, the latter mixed, according to Chamorro, with Colonial Baroque. The *gorra*, a cloth helmet with protruding flaps worn by the present women to stop them becoming as brown as Moors—worn together with gloves and stockings when working out of doors even in temperatures up to 40° C—was probably an invention of the Old Christians, though, as has been said, it is now worn by all girls and women, even those of the darkest hue.

Many of the rather fantastic place names—Jinijinámar, Triquivijate, for example—are of Moorish origin, but it is usually said that these are of pre-conquest importation. However, neither Giroldi's 1426 map nor Valentim Fernandes' of 1500 show such names, the words on them being all but entirely taken from common Spanish. Then, abruptly, on Torriani's map of 1590, when one would expect them, Moorish words appear: Hineguinama, Guadalique, and perhaps others. Further, modern villages with this sort of name occur all but entirely in the south-eastern zone of the main part of the island—and there is a 1595 record that the segregated Moriscos had the eastern half of Fuerteventura to themselves. Not one Moorish name settlement occurs in the choice zone, the Betancuria *barranco*; in fact a crescent of villages with Castilian names defends the approaches to the western cordillera. The capital of the northern end, the venerable La Oliva, ancient seat of the aristocracy, seems to have blocked the Moorish spread in that direction, for the villages up there are all of Castilian name. But, by counting the settlements with Moorish names along the eastern edge of the central plain, and in the eastern cordillera and lava-field, one can just reach the thirteen settlements of the chronicler. So a post-conquest origin for most at least of the Moorish place-names is probable. On the African coast opposite Fuerteventura, there is a place named Tarfaya, recalled not only by the Trequetefía cave but by a village at the foot of the eastern cordillera, Tefía.

The author also remarked in the modern island speech the curious prefixing to certain words of the Arabic article '*al-*'. This opens up a vast field of speculation. A great many now standard Castilian words are of course composites of the Arabic article and noun. For example, the current Castilian *almohada*, pillow. These composites are of course the legacy of the several hundred years' domination of the Spanish peninsula by Arabic-speakers, the last stage of which ended in 1492. But what of the occasional use of *alperdiz* for 'partridge' on Fuerteventura, when the current Castilian is *perdiz*; of *jorado* for the *Asteriscus sericeus* plant in Antigua, but of *aljorado* by a shepherd at Castillo de Lara just over the cordillera; of *pispa* by one shepherd, for the trumpeter bullfinch, of *alpispa* by another?

The island's Castilian began with that spoken in the fifteenth century on the Peninsula—with perhaps a few Aragonese and Leonese words—and survivals, lost on the Peninsula, could probably be traced in the islands; the Canaries are a survival region for all sorts of things. But the first example above, *perdiz*, is not of Arabic origin, and the other two, *jorado* and *pispa*, are not current Castilian. One is tempted to suggest that the last two have never been Castilian, and that they were probably imported direct from the nearby coast in the late fifteenth or sixteenth centuries. And that the habit of prefixing them by '*al-*' came with them, and that the Moors responsible applied the prefix to a number of words of the Castilian tongue, a language which, though initially incomprehensible, they have of course eventually assimilated—such a word being *perdiz*. Other examples of interest include the way the Castilian *apañar*, much used in the sense of 'to round up' when talking about the *gambuesas*, described later, often sounds more like *albañar*; whilst the hybrid *almejillón*, mussel, from the Arabic-origin Castilian words *almeja* and *mejillón*, is an obvious mixture to people who could stick an '*al-*' in front of the Castilian for 'partridge'. Some islanders even say the '*al-*' is optional!

It has already been noted, when discussing the Mahohs' speech, that the Arabs reached the African coast opposite by about AD 700. The linguistic result of this is that Arabic has supplanted Berber in many areas; however, parts of the adjacent coast now Arabic-speaking only changed over *in the fifteenth or perhaps sixteenth century*. The time of the Canaries' slave-catching raids, notably 1476 to 1593, was, then, just the moment to find people there who were ready to prefix '*al-*' to anything and everything. One can suppose that the captives of the Lord of Fuerteventura, about then more or less accustomed to the Arabic prefix, would, on arrival in the Canaries, be confused by finding it *apparently* in use in Castilian; however, more confusingly still, it was apparently only used with *some* words and then with a Castilian article *as well*, the words being in fact those of Peninsula-Arabic origin, many already known to the incoming slaves in West-African-Arabic. Presumably some imported Moors tried to use *both* articles with *all* Castilian words: *'el alperdiz'*! Corruption and hybrids, plus of course West-African-Arabic and Berber words—especially for plants and birds *recognised* by the enslaved Moors, for example the cited *Asteriscus serieceus* and the trumpeter bull-finch, also called *pájaro moro*—all are to be expected. Pronunciation too would for long be poor, and probably accounts for Glas' statement that the islanders of the mid-eighteenth century spoke 'barbourously'.

More valuable imports from adjacent 'Berbería' were the camel, still in use in the twentieth century, and *morisquillo* wheat, both fifteenth-century arrivals. The *morisquillo* grain was taken in one of Diego de Herrera's raids, and found to be much more prolific than the then current island grain—possibly of pre-conquest origin, but much more probably brought from the Peninsula—and also to be better suited to local conditions. At present two types of wheat are sown: a large-grain Peninsula import, and a small-grained local variety, called *morisco*, which yields less but is more able to withstand dryness. Fuerteventura's much used *gavias*, water-and-alluvium catchments, though probably of basically Arab origin, since they are used in Murcia and Almería, no doubt came via the Peninsula rather than direct from the African continent; the *noria*, or water-wheel, probably came by the same route.

The proportion of NW African blood in the present islanders must clearly be high, and physical comparison with the Tekna, Imraguen and other inhabitants of the adjacent continental zone would be interesting. On Fuerteventura two easily distinguishable groups have been described already: the square-faced evolved 'Mechta-Afalou' and the long-faced evolved 'Early Mediterranean'. The plates on pages 108, 126 and 143 include

96

members of a third group : they are the farming family, the shepherd and the saddlemaker. Four of these are of short, the other of medium height; their faces are tall and narrow but, apart from their low stature, this type differs from the others in the prominence of the mouth or alveolar region, a protuberance emphasised by the great distance between mouth and nose; alveolar prominence is a characteristic of the not otherwise very similar 'Orientaloid' type noted by anthropologists in Gran Canaria. These three extremes are fairly certainly amongst the descendants of the Mahohs who survived the 1405 conquest and of the Moors caught on the continent within the two hundred years which followed.

The Moors' last contribution to be noted is that they have acted and still act as whipping boys and butts of local humour, though this is common throughout Spain, of course—for example, they are still segregated on the Madrid to Algeciras trains. The breaking of an image in the Río Palmas hermitage, centuries ago, and to which a lengthy song is dedicated, was apparently the work of a *mora loca*, a mad Moorish woman. The *mimus* shrub is sometimes known as *venenero* or 'poisoner' . . . and sometimes as *tabaco moro*. Those who have been in Ifni and Spanish Sahara refer to the Moors with good-humoured contempt, but say it is dangerous to venture far from the predominantly Spanish capitals without a strong force. To be called a *moro* is the height of insults. There are no African nationals in Fuerteventura nowadays nor, a casual visitor would imagine upon hearing the way people talk, is there any African blood there either. It is thus ironical that the island's intermittent rich harvests, the *años buenos*, should have depended until today, not upon goat-horns or Christianity, but upon *morisquillo* wheat sown, much of it in Arab *gavias*, with the help of the Barbary camel, and kept irrigated by the *noria*, the Arab waterwheel.

6   ANCIENT RUINS

PPENDIX 3, listing sites of ruins, gives an idea of the extent
of the population around the time of the conquest. These
ruins survive because the incoming colonials and their
descendants did not live there, nor use the stone; most of these
sites would have been considered unattractive and inaccessible.
But how many pre-conquest dwellings must have been built in
the fertile valley beds beside the springs, and were thus obliterated
by more recent farms and villages? Yet many of the still existing
and thus undesirable sites are large. Even allowing for the prob-
ability that all the sites, both suggested above and listed in the
Appendix, were not inhabited at once, because of natural aban-
donment and seasonal transhumance, the population must have
been considerable. Abreu Galindo, writing in 1632, stated that
Fuerteventura had 4,000 fighting men at the time of the conquest, 1402–5.

Round to oval stone huts seem likely to be the earliest constructions, pre-conquest in style and often in origin, to judge
by the associated potsherds and stone tools. Rectangles, occasionally bay-ended, are probably the more recent ruins. Continued or renewed use of an ancient dwelling must have been
frequent.

The post-conquest slave-catching hunts in Africa, by increasing the ranks of the poor, must have gradually populated or
repopulated the least desirable areas, such Moriscos and their
descendants as could free themselves from bondage probably
opting for the tranquillity of otherwise inhospitable places; the
waterless, uncultivable Pezenescal Alto (W Jandía) may be an
example of such a settlement, now ruined.

98

One of Fuerteventura's earliest dwellings must be the Laguna cave. It lies on the northern side of the crater, being formed by a split in the skin of larva. The vertical rift has become choked by rough boulders fallen from above. At one point there is a gap or tunnel in the filling, an immense block has wedged itself across the crevice. A pyramid of animal bones, limpet shells and large and small fragments of Mahoh pottery rises up the steep flank of the volcano, its apex pointing at, reaching into the ill-shaped cave.

Once inside, the cave seems more like a warren than a dwelling. Tunnels, more or less choked with rubble and dust, twist away from the first chamber, burrowing out of sight amongst the boulders which have piled up in the rift. These tunnels go up and down : the floor is simply the tops of fallen blocks, the gaps between them filled with dust and bones, except right in the middle where a pit allows one to reach a lower level, from which more choked earthy tunnels spread in all directions.

Broken pottery lies everywhere. There are many fragments of what is perhaps the island's most primitive vessel. In shape this was a truncated ostrich egg. The near-oval pot was often decorated with incised lines, at their simplest consisting of a short line from which hung say five more, the clump repeated half-a-dozen times around the vessel, just below the rim. Sooner or later the ovoid developed a shoulder and, in the case of the milking pot or *tofio*, still just in use, a flat bottom and a spout. The clumps of incised lines, eventually spreading to entirely cover the bodies of vessels of all shapes, were always the potters' basic ornamentation, often with more delicate designs around the neck. Many other forms and decorations occurred; examples are a globular pot and the chevron and its derivatives. A detailed pottery study would be out of place here.

Under an overhang there lies a thin white disc carved out of the local travertine, one side flat and somewhat greasy, the other lightly domed, obviously a pot-lid; the travertine has been selected so as to include a pebble in it, and the carver has worked to leave a part of this sticking out, in the domed upper side, obviously as a knob with which to lift it.

In a corner there are two stone balls, about a kilo each. Outside, striking amongst the rough lava, a smooth-faced oval dish-quern has slithered some way down the side of the cone. Apart from a waste flake of white flint, all the stone tools are of black basalt, most of them broken cutters: flat strips, into which some of the island basalt fractures naturally and easily, one edge blunt, providing a finger rest, the other originally sharp but heavily chipped by use. Half a shell button or pendant, by design much like a miniature pot-lid, perhaps with two wide-apart thread holes when complete, lies on the little terrace at the cave's mouth.

A LAVA-FIELD DWELLING

The badlands of the central plain hold many once occupied shelters. Some are above ground, like an overhang in a Malpaís Chico lava hummock; the usual food remains and artifacts are embedded in the loose drifted ash in front. Others are below the surface, such as one Malpaís Grande dwelling in the spine of a petrified wave of lava. There is good visibility in all directions, even to the sea at Pozo Negro. The smooth ridge has split: the rift, nowhere more than three metres deep, is very much choked with fallen blocks. Amongst them a neat black hole is noticeable, leading through into a small cave. From inside it is clear that an overhanging edge of the rift has been carefully walled in; from outside the walling is invisible, hidden under loose rubble, perhaps deliberately. There is another larger entrance at the other end of the cave; both are well-shaped and lintelled with long flat stones. The dusty cave, not apparently used by animals, is littered with Mahoh pottery and stone tools, the latter of basalt and of two much rarer volcanic glasses, red and yellow. Large even for the Mahohs, the limpet shells are up to 9cm long. Having crawled

100

out of the den, the next stage is up the rift, stepping over potsherds, Mahoh and later, some wheel-made. As collapsed shelters succeed each other, it becomes clear that the rift was probably a small Mahoh settlement.

No doubt it was from badland dwellings like these that came the 50 Mahohs whom Gadifer fought unsuccessfully on the third reconnaissance. Others are the Laguna crater's cave; a dwelling cave and huts at Punta Goma, in the last lava-wave north and facing the Antigua plain; and at El Saladillo, on the coastal Pozo Negro fringe of the badland, a camouflaged hut-complex, one minute cell still with its slabbed, domed roof. Modern sherds are to be seen in all these, since, during the droughts, the shepherds try to find pasture in the lava-fields, spending a month there at a time, with just a blanket and the flock for company.

A HUT SETTLEMENT

Mention has already been made of the Risco del Carnicero mountain village, which overlooked Gadifer's way into the southern end of the Río Palmas valley. The settlement is best approached down the buttress which joins the narrow steep promontory to the western cordillera.

The ridge drops away and, at an abrupt turn, three brown domes erupt from its surface, barring the way ahead. Around these bare hummocks, their lower slopes lost under piled rocks over which have spread thickets of cactus and straggling *espárrago*, there hangs an atmosphere of primitive life. An immediate feeling that the place has been the scene of intense human activity, because, perhaps, under primitive circumstances one would choose to live there oneself. The bedrock of the paths which are automatically followed is polished and shiny with use, the overgrown spring comes as no surprise. Such too are the triple Megalithic towers of the Menorcan Talayots d'en Gaumés—just rocks, hummocks made of immense blocks, the wind racing over their summits. And the Roc St Christophe, a hundred-metre slot in the limestone cliff above the black, silent River Vézère in the Dordogne, its obvious yet easily-defended track worn smooth and now overgrown. At these places one can imagine the figures moving about, climbing slowly with heavy burdens, driving up animals, fighting and dancing, hear shouting and songs and the bleating of the flocks, see the smoke rising from the fires and the sunlight on the stripped earth.

Once again the choice of site suggests the Mahohs went in fear of attack. Although far from the coast, they chose a place which is sheer on three sides and only approachable along a narrow spine on the fourth. The central hummock alone seems to have been occupied. Its leeward, southern flank is naturally broken up into stepped, narrow terraces, and every possible space has been built upon, right to the summit—a length of perhaps a hundred metres, the lowest line of dwellings being about fifteen metres below the peak. The buildings, many sunk into clefts, are clearly traceable, at least twenty ruins still retaining some shape : circular, and only a little over a man's length in interior diameter. The height of the walls, some with small squarish recesses, is now beyond estimate. Blocks weighing a ton or more, almost certainly found where they were used, form the basis of the walling; where these were not available large well chosen stones, at their best each one straddling the two immediately below, have been used. The lintel stones to two entrances are still in position. On the highest terrace, in front of a narrow cleft in the summit of the brown hump, there is a much larger more important ruin, whilst higher still, just behind the very top and on the dark and windy northern side, there is a small cave with two entrances, clearly once occupied.

The vegetation is amongst the most dense to be seen on the island, mainly the golden flowers of the *jorado* and the paler, modest yellow of the *tabaiba*. Scattered amongst the rocks and the plants are gigantic wind-polished limpet shells, and here and there fragments of necklace plaques. The latter are usually made from a large thick-walled sea-shell now simply called a *caracol*, a species of *Conus*. Several plaques have broken across their holes, one during drilling; also, oddly, there are two perfect blanks. Fully shaped and smoothed, and still as strong as when newly-made, they have never been pierced : what happened that they were never finished?

It was near the ominously-named Butcher's Crag that, during the third reconnaissance, Gadifer made his first recorded contact with the islanders, capturing the three women for slaves in the 'flat and beautiful valley' below. When, the next year, the conquerors came to make their Valtarhais fortress higher up the fertile Río Palmas valley, they would not long have tolerated a settlement in a position commanding the pass. Possibly, bearing in mind their first visit, the Mahohs fled at once. Either way life on the hummocks probably came to an end suddenly. It takes a lot of rubbing to make a flat rectangle out of a snail-type shell— unpierced plaques would not be lightly discarded.

About half-way down the eastern cordillera the map marks 'El Esquén', implying that a Mahoh religious sanctuary or *'efeguen'* stood thereabout. The traveller asking the way will find that recent islanders have further corrupted the name to Lesque Ridge, Lomo Lesque. On a little plain just east of Montaña del Sombrero, and near a spring, a great circle of foundation stones may be the remains of the *efeguen*, perhaps dismantled by the Catholic missionaries.

No ruins of these have ever been found, but they are known to have existed because Galindo described them. This priest's work seems only to be known in Glas' translation, and this refers to the Mahoh sanctuary as an *'efeguen'*, also comparing it to the Shluh for priest, *fquir*. At present, and all over the island, there are place-names such as Esque, Esquén, Lesque and Lesquén, varying with past and present slurring and truncating pronunciation. The origin of these names would be even more obvious if one could show that Glas had mis-copied *efeguen* for *eseguen*; a true 'f' letter has been used by his printer. Even Montaña de Escanfaga may be 'the mountain of the *efeguen* of the brambles', an over-

103

grown sanctuary. Usually isolated, places with these names have never been systematically examined or excavated.

Each valley, each cluster of houses even, probably had its *efeguen*, the place where the Mahoh pleaded with and worshipped his conception of a supreme being. According to Galindo the *efeguen* was, from outside, nothing more than a tall strong circular wall with a very narrow entrance gap at one place only. Inside there was a second high wall, this time with its entrance at the opposite point of the compass to that of the outer wall. In the centre of the interior area there was a small table made of piled stones. There were little square recesses in the surrounding wall, and in them stood small earthenware pots holding offerings such as butter and milk.

THE JANDÍA WALL

The famous 'Megalithic' or 'Cyclopean' Wall, built, in pre-conquest times, right across the narrowest part of the island, the 5km wide Jandía isthmus, is one of those somewhat inaccessible relics which, since few chroniclers ever go to see them, grow mightily in stature and importance : though much dilapidated, the original width of the Jandía Wall is still clear, about a metre.

Having dealt with the 'Pasa Si Puedes' or 'Pass If You Can' cones by taking a track scratched along the face of the sea cliff, the traveller will find the waist-high wall just on the southern cliffs of the Beach of the Wall, as might be expected. In construction it is exactly like a Mahoh dwelling wall. The rocks have been collected off the surface, not quarried; the foundation stones are about half sunk in, by design or by drift pile-up. It hummocks away eastward, across the isthmus. The French found two unequally sized, warring kingdoms on Fuerteventura, one on either side of the wall.

Although they called the island 'La Forte Ventura', the name which first appeared on the 1339 planisphere of Angelino Dulcert, the French of 1402 also referred to it as 'Erbanne'. Somewhat incredibly it seems nowadays—particularly since they arrived in the summer, after the grass. However, it is said that when they asked one of the subjects of the northern realm what *he* called the island, the reply was 'my land', which sounded like 'Mahoh'. Others have said *mahoh* was the islanders' word for the flat hairy skin shoes they wore; more probably the shoes were only called that later, for they seem to have been used in other islands after the conquest, probably getting their name rather as has the English garment 'jersey'. Anyway, the name 'Mahoh' was applied initially to the northern realm, under King Guixe, in which the French landed. By Castilian writers it has come to be written 'Majorata', and it is interesting to speculate upon the reason for the pride with which the twentieth-century islanders of Fuerteventura call themselves *majoreros*. The southern realm, chronicled as Handía, now Jandía, was ruled over by King Ayora. The Wall was referred to by the pro-Bethencourt manuscript : 'There the land is of sand, and there is a great stone wall which crosses from one coast to the other.'

A SUMMIT FORTRESS

There is a reassuring lack of legends about the early people, and one feels both the intended truthfulness and probable accuracy of anything the present country-people say of them. Nobody brings them up, they do not profess to know a lot about them, and when they do discuss them it is solemnly and with an apologetically cautious '. . . or so they say' at the end.

On the lower slopes of the knife-ridged Monte Cardón, 593m, amongst the glossy brown boulders, there stands, here and there, an old whiskery shepherd, propped by his staff, much like a lone stem of the tall thin grey cactus long rooted in the mountain. All are of the opinion that the Mahohs lived on the extensive summit ridge in caves now strewn with human bones. Some will add that 'it was when they were being hunted, and they just stayed up there until they died of hunger'.

The northern heights, some 350m above the village, are separated from the central and highest stretch of the mountain by a steeply-sided notch, where a softer rock is being ripped away by the gale. This precipice is amongst the most striking on the island : a wall of magenta velvet criss-crossed by a network of raised black seams. Ash tuff with sills or dykes of basalt, as far as can be made out from a distance. Keeping to the north of this, the traveller climbs a ridge betwen two ravines; this turns into a steepish face. Limpets appear, and then fragments of decorated pottery, embedded in the earth. The climber covers the last of the scree and reaches the ridges and hummocks of the outcropping bedrock, here a mixture of brown basalt and consolidated grey ash.

There are perhaps twenty or thirty caves, all of them cut into the top of the face of the mountain's shoulder, some fifty metres below the summit, and burrowing down into the ash at the back of several narrow terraces in such a way that there is no sign of them to an observer in the ravines below. Two at least are five metres in diameter and tall enough for one to stand up in, but most have collapsed; some are now hardly large enough for a goat to live in. There are hundreds of potsherds, there has clearly been considerable occupation.

The top of the caves' outcrop is a narrow almost-level strip which, with a drop along either side, runs up against a wall of hard rock : the face of the final pinnacle and clearly not to be easily climbed. At the foot of it, in line along the flattish strip— which is only three metres or so wide—are the ruins of two stone buildings, partly sunken into the gale-torn surface. Edging round onto the eastern, shadowy side of the overhanging pinnacle, this is found to have been thoroughly fortified : each possible climb is closed at the top by carefully-made lichened walls. Not even a goat could have got up when the walls were complete, but now one has quite fallen and it is possible to climb up the rubble and onto what must have been the last retreat of a group of Mahohs, and one of the strongest of the island's *fortalezas*.

The citadel consists of a complex of narrow terraces around a jagged central pinnacle. The pinnacle is holed almost right round by caves, and these too contain pottery. 'They lived there . . . when they were being hunted.' In the fifteenth century this

Page 107: (above) Delivering water at Triquivijate, with the village church behind; (below) Camel and donkey team, ploughing, near La Oliva

Page 108: (above left) Half-profits worker irrigating a potato field; (above right) His wife—note her 'Early Mediterranean' face; (below left) Francisco and Primitiva Brito, farmers; (below right) Their son, Lorentiano, with typical island dog

final stronghold must have been secure against the invaders. To defend themselves and their women, children and animals, the Mahohs would have had throwing balls, stone fighting knives or *tafiaguas*, and the *tezeres*, their staffs-cum-lances, and their round shields. Another defence was the reluctance of the Europeans, less sure-footed, to venture into the mountains. The Mahohs can be visualised doggedly resisting siege up on their peak, going out at night onto their old pastures to cut plants for the emaciated goats, grubbing up truffles on the slopes where they had spent their lives, raiding the corrals of the conquerors—many of which hold their own animals—and carrying out attacks, to get food or to free prisoners or in revenge. 'We have come to make you Christians' was what the conquerors always replied when the ancient Canary people asked why they disturbed their land.

7   POST-CONQUEST ARCHITECTURE

SINCE the conquest, the bulk of the population has lived on the agricultural lands, that is to say the rambling central plain, a few fertile *barrancos*, for example, Río Palmas, and such other patches of alluvium as could be irrigated. In the first centuries after the Spanish colonisation, the inland position of the settlements was also in harmony with the perennial fear of invasion, particularly by the Moors. As in Lanzarote, significantly, the capital—Betancuria—was given the least vulnerable of sites. Each zone of the island was dependent on its own minute fishing port for communications and trade.

In the nineteenth century the appearance of the steamer coupled with increased security from invasion caused considerable change. As in Lanzarote, the old capital was abandoned in favour of the main steamer harbour, now called Puerto del Rosario but then Puerto Cabras; the steamer's other port of call, Gran Tarajal, became the second town. All the other coastal villages dwindled in importance and inhabitants, whilst the agricultural communities, though indispensable, began to stagnate, in increasing isolation.

CASA DE LOS CORONELES

Here and there about the Canaries there can be seen what the awestruck local people describe as a *casa señorial*, usually an ancient manor. In social standing next above the prosperous farmers, the occupants will have been those who spent their time proving, says Captain Glas, that 'there had never been a butcher, taylor, miller or porter' in their families, in the hope of ennoble-

110

ment. Usually such houses are heavily shuttered except perhaps for one small panel high above the ground. One wonders, in passing, who lives up in that dimly-lit room . . . perhaps a high-haired, black-draped crone who eats boiled beans beneath a mouldering portrait of Alfonso XIII.

The poorer part of La Oliva lies in the lava-field, the richer on the surrounding red alluvium. Upon the latter, towards the cordillera, stands the island's most august building : the Casa de los Coroneles, a *casa señorial* in the ancient Canary-Andalucian style, where the military governors, colonels, used to live. It was built in the eighteenth century, at a time when the inequality in the island incomes was a little more visible than it is now. A fine, solid old place, it is in decay, remaining empty most of the year, in the hands of people who do not live on Fuerteventura. The huge house, probably a square with an interior courtyard, has two storeys. The battlemented front corners, which must have struck awe into the often unruly islanders, enclose the main roof, long, sloping, of greyed orange tiles. The façade is a mature blend of yellow and red washes and, as any local will tell the visitor, its windows hold as many panes of glass as the year has days. Since perhaps half the islanders still do not have a single pane in their houses, and many not even a window, one can imagine the marvel that the Casa de los Coroneles must have been two hundred years ago. Its rickety wooden balconies, one to each upper window, are finely carved, and so is the great door. The stone around the door, and a sculptured coat-of-arms above, is richly overgrown with grey orchil.

George Glas has left an account of his visit to the house in the middle of the eighteenth century. He finds the Governor and his son 'sitting in a large hall, paved with flags, the sides of which were adorned with musquets, swords, and pikes. On my entry they received me in a distant but polite manner, and desired me to sit down'. Captain Glas avoids their attempts to involve him in religious disputes until after dinner 'soup made of oil, vinegar, water, pepper, and onions, with a few thin slices of bread; after this course came three boiled eggs, with tolerable good wine and bread'. Restored by his meal, he was then able to deal severely with his amateur inquisitors. His host eventually changed the subject and pointing to the array of arms 'most of which were grown rusty : he asked me if we had any so good in England'. Captain Glas does not record the answer he gave.

Nothing has been built near the Casa de los Coroneles except a farm, which probably supplied it. The earth-roofed, whitewashed house does not look occupied, and it is said to be haunted —things rise up of their own accord, voices are heard. Inside its courtyard is an immense eight-sided drinking trough carved out of a single boulder. On the empty plain behind the farm there is a spread of limpets and a few scraps of decorated preconquest pottery. Behind are the grey, ravined mountains, unchanging. Who haunts the farm? Guixe, the last King of the Mahohs' northern realm? One of the many eighteenth century *hechiceras* for whom the Island Council wanted a Witch House? A Moorish slave captured by an early Señor Territorial during one of the raids on the Barbary Coast? La Oliva is a very old place.

WATCH TOWERS

Amongst the earliest secular monuments still standing are two round, black defence-towers, one on the east coast at Fustes, an abandoned anchorage just south of Puerto del Rosario, the other at the north-western Cotillo, still active as a fishing community. The Cotillo tower is the one which, built about 1740 by Claude de Lisle as part of the defence plan of General Pignatelli, was mistaken by Major, Gravier and Olivia Stone, all writers of important late-nineteenth-century works, for Richeroque, the fortress built by Bethencourt halfway down the west coast, probably near El Saladillo, in 1404. Even now the Cotillo tower, like its twin at Fustes, is in usable state : a spiral of rooms, feeling like the inside of a snailshell, from which a curling staircase, in the wall itself, leads to the roof-top cistern and guard-house, the battlements beside the latter pierced with narrow shoots angled menacingly downwards onto the little drawbridge outside.

The two towers were put up as a protection against English

pirates and the like. Since the enemy could equally well land at any of a couple of dozen places, these immobile strongholds, two cannons and five men each, must have been simply to show good intentions on the part of the government, the islanders having made frequent appeals for protection; at best a fleeing boat could try to reach one of the two harbours. Glas reported that the 'Sergeant of the militia . . . is to alarm the island, and retire with his family and the crew of the barks, into the tower, and draw in the ladder after him, and shut the door : in which case I imagine it would be no easy matter to get at them'. Perhaps Captain Glas would have liked to have led the English pirates against Tuineje, a few years earlier. But a worse end awaited him. Released from the Tenerife prison, Glas was a passenger on a small ship back to England when the crew mutinied. The captain and two loyal seamen were killed even as Glas was fetching his sword. On the way back he was ambushed, disarmed, run through and thrown overboard, his wife and twelve-year-old daughter being flung after him alive.

FARMHOUSE

Wherever there is water and alluvium, a farmhouse will be found. El Cortijo Antiguo, probably one of the first to be built after the conquest, is famous for its pure water. Its plant and bird preserve has already been described.

The farmhouse, now only used seasonally, lies on the old Antigua-Betancuria *camino* over the cordillera, some way up a steep eastern ravine and below the peak to which it has given its name, Morro del Cortijo. Dominating the plain, it is approached up a rough track, a long winding scar in the cordillera flank's pink travertine skin. The farmhouse, squat and spreading, is an amber colour with a grey tinge caused by patches of stones left unfaced. The building has the shape of a right angle, facing across the *barranco*, with a single room standing free in the angle. The walk between is roughly cobbled, the stones shiny, the earth speckled with bits of red earthenware pots and with the mauves and blues of flowering agricultural weeds. A

113

domed bread-oven stands at the end of the lower arm of the building, against the kitchen. Using the back wall of the house, which is low because of the steep slope of the ravine, there is a long roughly built stable, leading to an open-air corral on the cordillera side of the farm. Two seats of loose stone, ears of young barley pushing up amongst them, flank the doorway to the main room, at the Antigua end.

Each room has only an exterior entrance; usually the houses begin with one or two rooms and the rest are added piecemeal as more and more related families come to live there. The roofs are made of beams, some chopped to rough shape, others just slender tree-trunks, across which lie closely-packed branches covered with several centimetres of ordinary island earth mixed with straw; the outer walls are stained by washed-off earth. The main room's roof has the branch layer replaced by a current substitute : hundreds of coñac-crate slats. Heavy rain saturates such a roof, with a danger of collapse, so that the tree-trunk props here and there are nothing unusual. The interior walls, one in the main room with a built-in cupboard, have been un-evenly faced with earth and straw which has then been white-washed. There is no laid floor, only the soft brown rock, crum-bling a little more at each step, pitted by heavy dripping and worn by uneven use into holes and ridges. Each room has one small window, which, made without glass, is closed by a shutter. The kitchen's ceiling and the upper half of its walls are black and glossy with caked soot. Right around the room, against the walls, there is a broad counter of rough stones; this is broken up by the cooking hearths, lit by a shaft of light, through a smoke-hole, directly above. The farmhouse's many dark corners and crannies shelter cockroaches and blackbettles, whilst gecko lizards prowl across the ceilings.

THE VILLAGES

As was to be expected of Jean de Bethencourt, he called the northerners' first settlement in the islands, the houses built by Gadifer's men around their fortress in Fuerteventura, by his own

114

name. Venerated for its place in the past, but otherwise now quite without importance, Betancuria, the island's ancient capital —and perhaps the first settlement in five or six hundred years of colonialism by European nations—lies in a shallow mountain bowl, about 400m above sea-level. Worn, barren ridges encircle it except to the south, where the water course along which the few houses are built disappears down a long valley, to reach the sea many kilometres away at Ajui, the little breaker-bound port which depended on Betancuria and so has long followed it into oblivion. The older houses of the abandoned capital recall the ancient farms of France and Spain, tall and with few windows, and with a silent permanent air.

Each of the ancient villages has its own characteristics. Below the Jandía's 807m Pico de la Zarza—the island's highest point— the houses of Morro Jable spread on to the sands, numerous yellow and green fishing boats drawn up amongst them; in the summer, many families migrate 'to the lighthouse', to a little settlement from which the tip's fishing grounds are easily reached. Antigua, sprawling over the plain, each of the low whitewashed houses with its peculiar view of the surrounding mountains, across a ravine, through palms, over a field of lucerne. Santa Inés, a silent, pale village built on a network of watercourses at the point where, in a confusion of slopes and channels, they all meet; the straw-coloured houses straggle along for a couple of kilometres, a few only visible at a time, the rest hidden by twists in the *barrancos*. Triquivijate, almost abandoned; against the sun, a shack on a hummock, with a single palm, as if cut in silhouette out of gold leaf; then, the gusts of wind sending glowing yellow dust flickering along the distant ridges, ruin after ruin, the amber walls almost visibly slipping and spreading, melting back into the throbbing plain.

THE PORTS

The whole windward or Barlovento coast of Fuerteventura, over 100km in a straight line, is now almost uninhabited, although it is the side facing the rest of the Canaries. Both steamer ports are on the African coast and the island is orientated towards them.

The two ports are much the most unattractive aspects of Fuerteventura. The steamer coming from Las Palmas calls first at Gran Tarajal; passengers go ashore in a launch because the shallowness of the harbour does not allow the steamer to tie up at the jetty. Examined from the deck, usually by the light of a pallid sun rising behind the ship, Gran Tarajal is seen to be a jagged grey mass of half-finished houses. Rectangles of undisguised cement, pocked with small square windows, they spread away up the bleak mountainside.

Puerto del Rosario, the capital, presents much the same picture on a larger scale. At the end of the quay a narrow waterfront offers a choice of the area of the barracks to the right and a muddle of dilapidated whitewashed houses to the left. In front of the latter there is a second but tiny jetty, usually green with weed and piled high with luminous web-like traps; here the small double-bowed fishing boats moor, and old men, back to the sea and the white sun, sit staring up at the huddled silent houses. Above these the traveller will find several large pompous public buildings, a poor market, the hotels and the few, limited shops. Further out the raw cement of the developing town stretches in all directions. The visitor passes through quickly, the interest lies beyond.

8   RURAL INDUSTRY FOR EXPORT

URING the centuries since the conquest, and in addition to the slaves and the goats, Europe has drawn on Fuerteventura for five products. They form a progression from the wild lichen shipped as collected to the cultivated sisal partially processed before leaving the island. The markets for orchil, barilla and cochineal, in all spanning actively 1405–1885, were each ended in the same manner, by artificial products. The sisal industry, dating only from the 1950s, appears handicapped by a low return and exterior competition. Tomato cultivation, only very recently begun in Fuerteventura in spite of its introduction into the Canaries in 1885, is booming; but the island's inescapable water problem is becoming worse.

ORCHIL

If it was the compass, rudder and map which made the conquest possible, it was the slaves, goats and orchil which made it worthwhile. The rubbery *orchilla* lichen (*Roccella tuberculata* var. *vincentina* and *R. fuciformis*) varies in colour from fawn to a dull mauve, is covered in white warts and grows in straggly tufts. It is at its best in damp crevices high up in the mountains, but can be found down to medium heights and on sunny rocks. In the higher parts it is often accompanied by *agicán* (*Ramalina siliquosa*, common in Europe), a lime-green lichen growing in tufts of flattish threads. The great attraction of orchil to medieval Europe was that it was a most valuable red and purple dyestuff.

Bethencourt came from Grainville-la-Teinturière, a village of dyers, where orchil would certainly be known, and the MS written in his favour notes that Fuerteventura 'once conquered

117

and converted to Christianity, this plant will be of great value to the lord of the country' and, later, that Bethencourt has decreed that nobody should touch the *orchilla* but himself. Soon after each island fell, and together with slaves and goats, the first cargoes of the lichen set off from its bays. The cloth of Europe was insatiable, the islanders' blood mattered less than a good dye. In 1438, the caravels of Henry the Navigator also stripped the uninhabited Salvage Islands of orchil, in order to satisfy the Portuguese demand for red and purple. In 1455 the Italian Alvise de Cadamosto recorded that 'orchil, skins, cheeses and fat' were then the main exports of the conquered islands. As fast as the big islands were conquered, towards the end of the century, orchil merchants established themselves at the pacified ports. Early in the 1500s, the Genoan agent Lerca concluded in Las Palmas three contracts in about as many days for a total of 120 *quintales* at 300 maravedis each, the purchasers to collect 'at any port, even on the west coast'—even dangerous loading conditions were worth it. Probably a hundredweight to a *quintal*, making six tons of lichen.

No wonder that, as time went by, it could only be collected at the risk of life : the island people had themselves let down the crumbling precipice faces in slings. The shepherds wore cloaks dyed emperor-purple, though the more humble unsaleable *agicán* was the commoner household dye. The latter, which gives a rich brown upon simple boiling with the wool, is much easier to use than the famous *orchilla*. The author, who has a Hebridean spinning and weaving workshop which uses plant dyes only, has never read a formula for orchil dyeing which would give results, since they have usually been written down by historians rather than by dyers. Here is the eighteenth-century Viera y Clavijo : 'Reduce to a paste, moisten, add a little slaked lime. This gives the colour of the flax flower, somewhat violet. But if first dyed a lightish blue, then the colour will be that of the flower of the rosemary, or of the pansy or of the amaranth. Again, the cloth first prepared with lemon juice, orchil will dye it a beautiful blue.' But it is not quite as simple as it sounds.

118

Nowadays, in all the islands as in Europe, lichen dyeing is finished, superseded by chemical products, often inferior but much cheaper. Only the very oldest of the people of Fuerteventura can remember when *orchilla* and *agicán* were used. Now both grow abundantly and accessibly.

BARILLA

Amongst the first wild plants to colonise the disappearing furrows of an abandoned or fallow field are *cosco* (*Gasoul nodiflorum*) and *barilla* (*Mesembryanthemum* [*Cryophytum*] *crystallinum*). Both are prostrate plants. The former consists merely of a slender jointed stem from which develop similar short branches, and is green with reddish tinges. The latter, though much the same colour, is far more showy, for it has thick curly leaves which are densely covered, like its stout stem, with glistening white blister-lets full of liquid. These xerophytes are at home in Fuerteventura, perhaps particularly so on the coast, since they enjoy salt-saturated soil.

Burnt, the island's wild glassworts yield a black cindery mass, known to Europeans of the past as barilla, from which can be extracted the soda needed by soap and glass manufacturers. Once a flourishing Spanish industry, barilla-burning had its northern parallel in kelp-burning. In Fuerteventura the barilla-makers were probably most active between 1750 and 1850. However, during the famines the plants' seeds were ground into *gofio*, and then the Fuerteventura Cabildo made sure that the hungry islanders got precedence over the spinning and weaving factories of England and Holland, some of the main consumers. By the end of the nineteenth century the chemical extraction of soda had much reduced the extent of the island industry. The poor people, however, went on making it for themselves well into the present century. The leaves burnt, a solution was made with the soft black mass, then the unwanted solids were strained off through a cloth : a liquid 'washing soda' was the result.

119

THE COCHINEAL INSECT

Like rather flattened blackcurrants, the swollen females, ready to be picked, occupy the centre of the colony; their legs have atrophied, they seem to have become just sacs of red-black liquid. Towards the perimeter of the mass they become smaller, until those on the outskirts are somewhat like minute flat woodlice; they have legs still, and are moving restlessly, waiting for a chance to get nearer the centre, to lay eggs and, in turn, die. The little swollen motionless bladders already in the choice position are sitting upon the unhatched eggs and old empty capsules, black on the white, powdery patch. The few males almost pass unnoticed; in shape they are rather like greenflies, but have white wings and pinkish bodies which end in two long, tail-like bristles. They crawl here and there across the hard-packed mass. The whole colony only occupies the centre of a single leaf.

The dried and powdered bodies of the females of *Dactylopius coccus*, the cochineal insect, are said to have built the Las Palmas Opera House, such were the riches brought by the nineteenth century's need for scarlet, crimson and orange dyes. Introduced into the islands in 1825, against active resistance by farmers who feared it would kill off the racquet-leaved *Opuntia* cacti upon which it lives and feeds, by the middle of the century production was about half a million dry kilos per annum, at 150,000 bodies to the dry kilo. But the 1862 London Exhibition included chemical dyes, and at once there was panic in the Canaries. In 1863 the laboratory colourings were shown to be fugitive, and the islands rejoiced. The showy horses, the jewellery, the wagers on the cockerel fights, all seemed safe. Alas, from 1868 the acceptance of poor dyes and short-lived fabrics—which has continued to the present—made itself more and more felt. By 1885 large-scale exploitation of the bug was uneconomical. When, round about 1900, it was found that both the tomato and the banana would grow well in the Canaries, capital embraced the new booms. Cochineal became reduced to a family affair, only worthwhile where labour is otherwise unemployed—as in Fuerteventura, where the banana can never grow for lack of fresh water and the tomato is only a recent introduction. The latest figures available for production of cochineal in the Canaries are the average for the years 1954–7 : a mere 15,000 kilos.

Nowadays, in Fuerteventura at least, cochineal-raising cacti are no longer planted—but the old plantations, though much deteriorated for lack of care, are still worth exploiting. This is now usually women's work. The only tools needed are a few scraps of muslin, a tin can on a stick, and a sieve.

The first thing used to be the planting of the racquet cactus, either the long-leaved *blanca* (*Opuntia maxima*) or the much rounder-leaved *colorada* variety; the *tuna india* (*Opuntia dillenii*), which grows equally well in Fuerteventura, is unsuitable, if for no other reason than because its rather smaller leaves are covered with very long spikes. The cochineal bug does not like the cold, nor long rain, nor frequent atmospheric change, whilst the two suitable cacti will grow where there is fair heat, little water and shallow though fertile soil : the mountain terraces and *barrancos* which fringe the great central plain of Fuerteventura are thus tolerably suitable for both, though parts prone to strong winds and intense heat have to be avoided.

To start off, leaves cut from other plantations are half-buried in the ground about two metres apart. The bugs can be introduced onto the growing plant after two years, but preferably at about five, when the plantation is clearly under way. The grafting takes place in April or May, to get in a full summer's harvests. A muslin bag containing a little 'white powder', the eggs, from another plantation, is pinned to each leaf : within a day or two a number of hatched bugs will be found upon the host cactus. Although new plantations are not now started, such transferring is still done around the old ones. Following their installation in the spring, the bugs grow fast, and three harvests can be made, at six-weekly intervals, before the winter brings the season to an end.

The harvesting scoop, funnel-shaped, is made from a beaten can and a palm stick : with it 3kg of fresh '*granitos*', the females, can be collected daily. Taking care to choose only the fat ripe ones, they are scraped or scooped off the leaves. The bugs have to be harvested or the leaves get 'burnt'; otherwise there is no danger to the cactus. In the good old days the first crop of each year, the best, used to be transferred to the bare leaves, but now short-term gains are the aim.

After collection, the bugs have at once to be killed since, removed from their food supply—the cactus—they will otherwise begin to eat each other. In Fuerteventura the massacre is done by spreading them on an outside cement floor or a sack and mixing in cold ashes, leaving the mixture in the sun for about eight days. The process is complete once the bugs have gone dry and hard. In order to increase the weight some people have been known to kill the harvest in cement. Once dead, the bugs are separated from the ash by sieving. They are now only about a third of their original weight.

The bulk of the Fuerteventura harvest is purchased by a Las Palmas firm, and their price appears to vary with their needs: from 90 to 250 pesetas a dry kilo, with the present price at 200 pesetas. However, the islanders are up to dealing with this, and withhold their bugs until the company's price is forced to rise. Such a chaotic system is typical of the marketing in the islands. 'They'—the middlemen, the bulk consumer, the wholesaler, the exporter—are the adversary, if not unscrupulous, at least unreliable. With 10,000 kilos of raw dry cochineal a small factory could be started actually on the island. Present consumption is in the dyeing of eastern silks, and, since cochineal is not poisonous, in pharmaceutics, lipsticks and food and drink colourings, and the consumers are Iran, Spain, the UK and the USA.

Vast uncared-for plantations can be seen around Antigua, sprawling lines of the long-leaved *blanca* cactus. It is obvious that the *granitos* and *bichitos*, the females and males, have to look after themselves; presumably their eggs naturally survive the winter, to hatch the next year. Only then does somebody appear to harvest them: 200 pesetas a day is well worth it. The hillside is not wanted for other cultivation. Although the eggs

122

can get blown about and the bugs can move to another leaf, few probably do shift voluntarily, for only one racquet in fifty has its colony; so it seems probable that they decrease if left to themselves. But, on the white-patched tenanted leaves, the little black blobs and the pinkish crawling flies are still busily living and dying, unaware both of their own present unimportance and of the achievements of their more illustrious ancestors.

SISAL

Linking the huts and plots of the poorer part of La Oliva, dusty *caminos* criss-cross the lava-field about which they are scattered. Due south of the Arena cone stands a signpost : 'Government Fibre Plantations—Experimental Cultivation'. It points towards the crater, up a grit track flanked on each side by a row of dull green-blue cacti, each one simply a bunch of sword-like fronds, points upwards.

The agave, or century plant, usually the common *'pita'*, *Agave americana*, is to be seen all over Fuerteventura. Everybody has a few growing, some boundaries are marked by impassable lines of them, the fronds serve as emergency animal food, the 8m seed-stalks make lightweight beams suitable for stable roofs. Many country people extract the fibre to make string and rope for their own use. In the 1950s it was decided to try to grow agaves seriously on Fuerteventura, thus giving people work both in the plantations and in the processing. Particularly around La Oliva, the results are striking : vast level spreads of ash, red to black, on which bristle ranks of green and blue agaves, their alignment impeccable in all directions. Seen from the surrounding mountain tops the spiky ranks change into blocks of green, runnelled with straight black shadows. Satisfying, blemish-free, an example of cultivating with the environment instead of, as for centuries, in spite of it.

The agave, combining certain growth with ease of cultivation, has clearly few rivals amongst the island's exploited plants, particularly as a long-term investment. Fuerteventura has always had vast stretches of flat fertile ground which have not been cultivated for lack of water, and the state plantation has acquired many of those around La Oliva. The agave seems to be able to grow anywhere hot, and does not need much moisture. But for best results it is grown in Fuerteventura in volcanic ash. Such cultivation is not however limited to the agave, but the preparation of the ground is costly : according to the 1950 Plan Chamorro it was then about 40,000 pesetas the hectare.

According to the crop to be grown, for example onions, maize or agaves, so the cleared, levelled land is first manured and then coated with a depth of between 7 and 20cm of fine volcanic ash. The latter is only quarried from certain volcanoes, not all being suitable; it used to be brought to the fields on camels—from an otherwise inaccessible quarry high up in the flank of the Gairía Crater, for example—but the government plantations have their own huge new Pegaso lorries. The magnificence of many cones has suffered from the colossal holes dug in their sides, but then the ash is amongst the island's few natural resources.

The roots of the young agaves are embedded in the earth beneath the ash. The coating of *picón* has two connected purposes : to avoid daytime evaporation of the moisture in the soil below and to attract and absorb—by reason of its spongy texture —the moisture in the night air, which adds itself to that preserved in the underlying earth. This is enough to produce a healthy agave, and the plant can now be left to itself for at least two years. The sponge effect of the ash may last as long as twenty years, but most coatings need refreshing after about five, weathering and dust causing it to lose its absorbent texture.

The common, often wild, *pita* agave, large and blue-grey, is not planted commercially; nor is its elegant yellow-margined variant, *A.a.* var. *marginata aurea*, also to be seen in Fuerteventura and probably a garden escape. The two commercial species are *henequén*, *A.fourcroydes*, and sisal, *A.sisalana*; at La Oliva, *A.zapupe* has also been tried but not pursued, having no particular advantage over the others.

The *henequén* plant varies in colour, being a mixture of dull

124

Page 125: A pause during a *gambuesa*, the monthly round-up on common grazing, at Fuente de las Ovejas, on the east coast.

Page 126: Salvador Santana, a shepherd, making cheese in a mould of plaited palm. Wind-driven pump behind

shades of green, blue, and grey. Every frond has small hard black prickles along each edge and a long black terminal spike. From 4 to 6 years old the harvesting begins, by cutting off the lowest fronds; at La Oliva, 26 are taken from each plant annually, weighing about half a kilo each, though two cuttings at six-monthly intervals will rather increase the total which the plant can lose without damage to it. It will live from 10 to 25 years, then seeding and dying. The seed-stalk is a startling thing, like an asparagus but as tall as eight metres. Upon the ends of the short high arms form both seed pods and bulbils, the latter being complete young plants; both fall to the ground and, amongst the suckers which have pushed upwards from the roots of the parent plant, attempt to take hold. But the ash keeps them from the earth, and propagation of all species is anyway done with plants reared in the plantation nurseries; the suckers, seeds and frustrated bulbils get removed with the weeds.

The sisal, origin of the well-known fibre, is dark green. There is a variety with prickles, but at La Oliva the smooth-edged plant is preferred; both, however, have the terminal spike, dark chestnut in colour. Sisal is altogether more delicate than *henequén*, resisting severe drought less well, yielding less fibre per annum and living only 5 to 10 years. But it can be cut at from 2 to 4 years old, its lack of prickles makes it cheaper to process, and its fibre is a better quality. Sisal only reproduces itself by suckers and bulbils. Only sisal is now planted, it having been decided that its advantages make it a better proposition than *henequén*.

Henequén or sisal, each plant's centre is 2m50 from that of each of its neighbours: 1,600 to the hectare. In the case of sisal the 26-leaf harvest weighs 11kg, or about 17 tons from each hectare. However, the dry-weight of the fibre extracted from this will only be one-twentieth. The processing is done in a series of white-washed buildings and enclosures actually in the lava-field, just below the black crater of Montaña Arena.

An engine chugging, and a medicinal smell, not unpleasant, comes from the low stripping building. Inside, in a long cool

H

shadowy room, six machines are in use; at each stands a man in overalls, sleeve guards, rubber gloves and rubber boots. Behind the operators there is a mountain of severed agave limbs—the fronds just as they leave the plant except that, as these are henequen, the fringing spikes have been slashed off, a job which has to be done by hand. Each man has a small heap of the prepared fronds beside him. Holding only the tip of the frond, he feeds the other end into the stripper's shrieking slot, rather like the jaws of a stamp machine, but whirling at terrific speed. The pitch of the racket becomes higher. Halfway in only, the morsel is withdrawn, and the machine is seen to have reduced its half of the frond, originally stiff, fat and juicy, to a limp tassel of pale green, sticky fibre. The operator turns the frond round, lets the machine chew the other half, then tosses the stripped 80cm hank aside, and reaches for another fresh frond. Already the fibre is recognisable : it is thick, hairy, creamy-white parcel string, the sort which comes unknotted of its own accord.

A different man now collects up the latest stripped heaps, and washes them in a large sink. Another man takes them from him, in a wheelbarrow, and pushes them out of the machine-room and into one of several drying enclosures. Here the hanks are spread out, thickly, on racks made of concrete legs and the long *pitones*, seed-stalks of dead agaves. A brilliant white in the sun, the lines of fibre with their bitter smell and hairy texture are as satisfying a sight as a fine bale of fleeces to a sheep farmer. Once dry they are hand-combed across a heavy, toothed board to get rid of impurities and to roughly align the fibres. A further man collects up the dried hanks—about four days in an average sun is long enough—and wheels them along to the packing department. The fibre is not processed any further on Fuerteventura, but simply sold in bulk to factories outside. So, once it has been made into bales and roped up, it is finished.

The superintendent is of the opinion that the plantation is proving a success. But the secretary of the La Olive *ayuntamiento* feels it is a failure. Other opinions are divided, depending on who is asked.

The plantation gives pleasant easy work to 60 men, and to them the enterprise must be a great success. However, until they got the machines, there were 200 workers. The superintendent would like more mechanisation, raising the question of whether the aim is to make money for the state or to give employment. He says the plantations—there is also a minor one near Antigua —are still an experiment. Perhaps once financial independence is reached they will be able to expand and take on more men again.

However, part of the general scheme is to encourage independent farmers to take up agave cultivation, their harvests being sold to the state plantation. But, since the farmers receive only 40 centimos a wet kilo of cut fronds, the work and capital seems insufficiently rewarded, even for Fuerteventura. Henequen or sisal, a hectare irrigated with ash, costing 40,000 pesetas to do as long ago as 1950, and which yields nothing the first two to four years, will even nowadays produce only 7,000 pesetas per annum when under way. A mature acre thus yields the independent cultivators the equivalent of about £18 a year. They cut the fronds in the winter, especially after rain . . . they weigh more then. Some say that the plantation doesn't *always* buy, and so crops have been wasted, and they're certainly not going to replant. It's like, they say, that cotton-growing nonsense which 'they' persuaded us to try, when the market was uncertain one year and the crop failed the other. Nevertheless, the superintendent of the agave plantation says that he takes everything that's offered him.

There is competition from East Africa and also from synthetic fibres. Will the island henequen and sisal go the way of orchil, barilla, cochineal, each superseded by a laboratory product? Four hundred hectares are now planted, about half henequen and half sisal. Annual total output is now about 150 tons of dry fibre, all consumed in Spain, and production is steadily increasing. At present both fibres, the henequen and the finer-quality sisal, sell at the same price, about 18,000 pesetas a ton. A mature acre yields £35 a year. A 1964 island workers' conference called

129

for a factory to make finished articles from the raw fibre, rather than export it. The frond residue has been used as tomato fertiliser, but apparently without much enthusiasm, to judge by the green ridge of rotting pulp below the building. If a way can be found to get rid of an acid it should be possible to make *aguardiente*, liquor, from the pulp, just as in Central America, where the agave originated, the spirits *pulque* and *mescal* are made from it.

But, in spite of all these possible uses, there is no sign that the agave cactus is to be the basis for another boom. Perhaps for this, the idea has come a hundred years too late.

TOMATOES

In surprisingly remote *barrancos* one can come across a tractor reclaiming land for tomato cultivation. Lurching along one of the broad grey-weathered ridges which divide up the watercourse into channels, the machine is cracking up the island's stony skin, ploughing it deeply to a rich earthy brown. Tomato growing, introduced into the Canaries in 1885 by an Englishman, has recently spread to the island, and considerable areas are now being turned over to it.

The capital needed is high, apart from purchase and reclamation. The land the tomato gets is usually poor, and a hectare requires an annual dressing of 6,000kg of chemical fertiliser and as much again of manure. Although salty water is used, even this is often deep, and some wells reach 150m; as long ago as 1950 a 100m well could cost about a million pesetas to sink. Fuerteventura, like the other islands, starts planting its seedlings in June, to catch the northern markets in winter and spring; planting out is in July, flowering two months later and picking, whilst green of course, starts after another month. Plenty of work is provided : ploughing, planting, sulphurising and fertilising, pruning, sticking and tying-up, weeding, constant watering. After planting, and in order to conserve the soil and the moisture, the surface of the plantation is coated with a thick layer of beach

130

or *barranco* shingle. A hectare holds 25,000 plants and yields 37,500kg of tomatoes, of which 70 to 85 per cent are within export standards. In the late 1960s the grower received about 6 pesetas a kilo, which would be some 190,000 pesetas the hectare; one plantation mentioned a sudden fluctuation up to 14 a kilo. Fuerteventura harvested six to twelve million kilos in 1959, and production has increased since then. Below-standard fruit probably now amounts to between one and two million kilos annually, and it is not surprising that one sees tomatoes spilled across the tracks and trampled upon, for the population cannot possibly eat them all: obviously, once the fishing fleet is improved, a tomato- and fish-canning factory could be started. Of the tomatoes exported from the Canaries, where probably about 10,000 hectares are now planted, Great Britain takes three-quarters. A boom to the poverty-stricken islanders, they and the plantation owners share between them about *two new pence* a pound, gross; this is disproportionately low at the side of the European growers' return. And yet tomatoes are far harder to grow in the Canaries than anywhere else.

Orchil, barilla, cochineal . . . and now the tomato. This fourth boom is yielding as much as its dead ancestors, but will it last? Chemistry ended the first three. Furteventura's export price cannot exceed that of the Canaries in general—with which a West African country, with plenty of fresh water, could anyway come to compete—so that above-average increases in Fuerteventura's irrigation costs could end the boom for the island. And, in fact, the level of the water-table of Fuerteventura is undoubtedly dropping, as the disappearance of streams and drying up of wells shows; will more and deeper drilling keep pace with this? Will not salinity, already at or near maximum in the case of the tomato wells, increase as the water is drawn from deeper and deeper down? Nowadays a tomato field, after two crops without heavy cleansing rain, is too saturated with salts to yield a third. The growers can always change to other ground, there is plenty of it; but this often involves purchase, often reclamation, well-sinking, removal and re-installation of the old plant, and so on, and costs are increasing all the time. Capital may soon turn towards something else, more and more to tourism, for example, and Fuerteventura's tomato boom may pass its peak. But at the moment the tomato vines are still spreading over the island. Like the end of a triumphant documentary, the tractor rumbles and reels along the uneven ridge, the sun setting behind it. Man, says the invisible commentator, is once again dominating nature. Only the geologists are pessimistic.

9   *THE WATER PROBLEM*

W ATER, or rather the perennial lack of it, has always dominated Fuerteventura. And not only is there the chronic shortage, but part of the supply is undrinkable and often unfit for irrigation too. Water is primarily responsible for the incomes, health and attitudes of the islanders.

Fuerteventura, an island desert, is clearly unable to sustain much human life. There are now about 18,000 inhabitants, and they are there in spite of the conditions. The 1744 census totalled some 10,000 people; it has been noted that Galindo claimed there were already as many as '4,000 fighting men' in 1402–5. Perhaps the first immigrants lived well enough : at least a thousand years earlier, say a few score people moving their flocks round and round the island, not over-grazing as at present, and sowing a few particularly damp, fertile patches of alluvium. There may even have been something worth hunting, like the wild pigs of Gomera and the giant lizards of Hierro. Now the island offers only a few sparse dwarfish plants as food for the domesticated animals. The despondent silhouette of the all but useless *mimus* symbolises the hopelessness of the barren land.

DRINKING WATER AND IRRIGATION

Probably typical of Fuerteventura's wells, popularly a thousand in number, is the one in the middle of Betancuria, sunk in the *barranco* bed below the houses. Covered by a stone construction key-hole-shaped in plan, the top of the cobble-faced shaft is reached along a narrow, thick-walled passage. A tall thin olive-

133

FUERTEVENTURA
POPULATION DISTRIBUTION AGAINST
SIMPLIFIED PHYSICAL CHARACTERISTICS

●   Major settlements

○   Minor settlements

▨   Mountains

▨   Lava badlands and craters

☐   Plains and main barrancos

▨   Sand waste

*ATLANTIC
OCEAN*

N

0   5   10   20 km

oil tin serves as a lifting bucket. *'Mejor agua en el mundo no hay'*, say the villagers—there's no better water in the world, a belief only to be put down to long conditioning and lack of choice. The taste of the water is both sweet and salty at the same time, with a hint of the texture of castor oil, the exact flavour varying with the food one is eating. Many of the wells are in fact so much suffused with mineral salts, up to seven grammes the litre, as to be undrinkable even to the islanders.

Various noteworthy island water sources have already been described. Perhaps the most bizarre of Fuerteventura's wells is the Fuente de la Marea, or Tideline Well, on the leeward Jandía coast. Sunk into the back of a beach and about 12m deep, certainly below sea-level, its water is perfectly tasteless.

Drinking water is traded, transported by lorry. Small quantities, down to casual drinks, are dispensed from tapped barrels carried on the backs of camels. For storage of the occasional rain-water—considered insipid—some have built cisterns, especially those living on deep permeable lava, well-less. As a last resort, drinking water is brought to the island in cistern-ships by the Spanish Navy.

The irrigation problems of the tomato plantations are common, as a generality, to all island agriculture. In addition to the temporary sterility often imposed on the soil by two tomato crops' irrigation during unbroken drought, there is the ominous fact that some wells have *become* too salty for any use at all, apparently even for first-crop watering of the tolerant lucerne and tomato plants, and have been totally abandoned. The big investors attracted to tomato cultivation are able to sink wells to 100 to 150m and thus follow down the water-table whose fall, by incessant exploitation, they are accelerating. However, the small farmer, equipped only with the Arab *noria* or animal-driven water-wheel, suffers at an equal pace, as his well refills ever more slowly and its maximum level drops steadily and for good. There is an improvement on the *noria*, the wind-driven water-pump—also, however, limited in working depth—coupled with a reservoir. Loans are available for well-sinking and for lifting gear, but the hazards of island farming make regular repayments difficult, or so they say.

The government has built reservoirs, for example at Río Palmas, but, inevitably becoming dry in the drought, the great heat cracks them up. A complaint is that the state makes too many roads—but then these, easy to make, do give work—and not enough wells. Official prospections are said to have been carried out in the late 1960s, seemingly to great depths, but it is hard to see how these could be used for the public good without a perennial state subsidy. Generally, island farmers feel deprived of national aid.

The irrigation system of a potato field, which yields crops all the year round, can be taken as an example of the extreme care used to ensure that not a drop of water is wasted. The plants grow on ridges 2m long in the centre of tiny enclosures; the enclosures, a few ridges to each, are in two long lines on each side of a central canal. The moving of a common canal-enclosure earth baulk through a right angle—done by a quick drag with the adze—both opens the enclosure and closes off the lower stretch of the canal. The terrace being prepared so as to slope, the water wastes no time in racing along the canal and into the proffered enclosure, which is shut off once it is full. There are no permanent constructions, nothing but ridges and channels in the earth.

EL AÑO RUIN

Go into any village shop-cum-bar and the chances are that, no matter the season, a couple of tables will be taken up by quartets of lackadaisical card-players, their movements mechanical. One or two other middle-aged villagers watch uninterestedly over their shoulders; they stand as if about to go, but rarely do. Unshaven, in stained black hats and patched clothes, these lean, silent men are farmers and, as usual, it is 'a rotten year'.

'*Es un año ruin*', they say again and again, a phrase which, because of its extraordinary currency, must merit a place on the island's coat-of-arms. 'It's a rotten year,' for it hasn't rained again.

After several rainless seasons few are bothering to plough and sow, it may not rain this year either . . . playing cards passes the time of day. Modern methods, different crops, new crafts, none are thought worth trying—the only change ever made is that to a town life—for it is soon clear that there is a deep-rooted feeling amongst the country people that nothing they personally attempt will succed, *el año ruin* is peculiarly theirs.

The pessimism and apathy of the common islanders begin far back in their past. Their ancestors were for several hundred years and until not long ago a slave-cum-serf class mainly composed of the conquered people and of captured Moors; ever since the conquest most of the best land has been in the hands of a few rich families; and there is a strong sense of isolation caused by neglect by the Peninsula-seated government. But, leaving all these reasons aside for the moment, a basic cause of the apathy and pessimism seems likely to be the centuries of poor nutrition suffered by the islanders. Here first is a Fuerteventura *año ruin* in the late eighteenth century, described by an eyewitness, the historian Viera y Clavijo. 'The stricken inhabitants abandoned their sterile land . . . consumed by thirst and hunger, waves of them disembarked like locusts in Gran Canaria and the other islands . . . the boats which used to return from Fuerteventura full of barley and wheat now brought cargoes of starving refugees, men, women and children . . . in order to come they had sold their inheritances for nothing, after watching their best animals die . . . it was terrible to see so many ragged homeless people crying out for bread in the streets. . . .'

Such extremity is now past, but, in the words of an enthusiastic yet much-frustrated government agricultural adviser, 'the islanders have the habit of living without many vitamins, without green foods and much else that's essential . . . if it doesn't rain, then they just sit and wait, often for years, somehow surviving, thanks to those goats'. But green vegetables and fresh fruit are scarce, though there is now a tomato glut, those unexportable. The Canary banana is hard to obtain and expensive, to the island housewife's fury. For lack of water there are no Fuerteventura bananas, but even in Gomera, with its vast plantations, to get a banana in a shop is a major feat, the UK, Denmark and other countries taking them all. The few sent to Fuerteventura—'too ripe or blighted for them to export'—have an average shop price of 12 pesetas a kilo, two or three times the grower's receipts on the nearby islands. At one-seventh the legal minimum daily wage and perhaps one-tenth the poorer class's maximum, bananas are the *cheapest* fruit available. Except during the local fig season; but, from unpruned water-lacking trees, the figs are small and dry. Green vegetables are usually limited to a few cabbages at 16 pesetas a kilo : two and a half cabbages for the minimum daily wage. In the *años ruines*, most years that is, there are sufficient vegetables and fruit only for the rich.

The agricultural adviser adds that 'if it rains then the fertile ground produces huge crops, it's an *'año bueno'*, they can't harvest it all and they get very rich, even with their primitive methods'. Yet it has never been easy for the islanders to derive any permanent advantage from the good years; these, nowadays in particular, seem anyway few. After the rare good harvest, the island farmer has always had the choice of selling his surplus at once to the other islands—with the market glutted and prices low—or of stock-piling. The latter, however, was, from the farmer's point of view, frequently disastrous : as soon as the *año bueno* gave way again to general hunger, the authorities would make a compulsory low-price purchase order. The following extract is from a report of the island Council, written at a 1789 session—there was an absence of cake in more places than France—and it is informative in many ways.

'Half-a-dozen farmers and merchants have some wheat to spare. As they are afraid that it may have to be shared out, and they aren't allowed to send grain out of the island, they are sowing it or exchanging it for animals or lending it or making any deal to appear not to hold it. The people have no money to buy it, and the owners might not sell it to them anyway, for often the sharing-out can only be done with violence. Luckily it has rained and there is plenty of pasturage, and so there's some milk—otherwise many would have died, even though the Bishop did sell some of his Privilege Grain. So we ask that the prohibition on sending out grain be maintained until the end of March, when a harvest is in sight. Still, had the little loan requested last June been granted, twice as much could have been sown. . . .'

A hand-drawn cartoon pinned up in the boat company's office in Puerto del Rosario in 1967 shows that the basic position is not much changed nowadays. The drawing depicted a small, laden trading-boat sailing away, 'Foodstuffs for Africa' written on its sails; a caricature figure, no doubt recognisable to the islanders, is just stepping aboard, whilst a man on the shore is bellowing : 'Godfather So-and-So, if it doesn't rain this year we'll just have to burn the *Seagull* !' It is clear that the average islander's purchasing power is still so low that the local food-producers try every means to export their produce to better markets. Putting the mass of the islanders in a still worse position, of course. To avoid this, the authorities have taken measures to discourage the export of foodstuffs.

The infrequent *año bueno* is simply not good enough to be spread over the bad years which all but inevitably follow. Unable to forecast their duration, those who have put aside grain and money live as frugally as those who have not been able to do so, partly as an insurance against prolongation of the drought or a fresh calamity like illness, partly because the habit is engrained in every islander.

RELIGIOUS FATALISM

When it does rain, and torrents of muddy water rush down the ravines, on their way to the sea, the country children are to be seen splashing about excitedly in the puddles; to any passer-by they shout : *'Ahora corre, ahora corre!'*—now the *barranco*'s running ! The birds sing. Yet many of the villagers are determinedly undemonstrative, seemingly loath to show any pleasure at the rain. Silently, sack-protected, they methodically open and shut section after section of their irrigation networks. Even a few hours' rain, if it soaks down, will however mean better pasturage for a month or so, more water in the wells, and perhaps a pea crop, though it may come too late to sow wheat or to save the year's barley fields. A second Deluge, like that of Noah, which some islanders say probably caused the fossil shells in the high coastal terrace, this alone seems likely to bring even a grudging hurrah from the people of Fuerteventura, who are most at home in an *año ruin*.

Allied to the lack of food, there are other causes for this morbid attachment, part of the spiralling hopelessness of the situation. As Aldous Huxley wrote of another materially backward land : 'India will never be free until the Hindus and the Moslems are as tepidly enthusiastic about their religion as we are about the Church of England.' There is no difference between 'the Will of Allah' and *'Si Dios quiere'*—if God wishes. Deeply-rooted fatalism is certainly not one of the many possible parents of invention. 'Sterility and hostile harvest-time weather again this year, despite the many petitions to Divine Majesty for enough rain for the sown fields and the animals, unanswered due to our faults.' 'The earthquakes of March and April being interpreted by the Cabildo as warnings by Divine Justice for our faults, the image of Our Holy Mother shall be taken out. . . .' 'In view of the locust plague the people are asking that the *fiesta* in honour of St John the Baptist should be renewed.' These are Cabildo minutes of the eighteenth century, though they could be of the twentieth. Following rain, the people of Antigua and two nearby villages sometimes unite their images, Saints Roque, Isidro and Francisco, and carry them in procession to and fro across the plain, both as a thanksgiving and as a request for a further downpour. But, for most of the time, the pitiless drought, and other calamities, go on as before. The inevitable result is a fatalistic attitude : nothing has ever succeeded and nothing ever will, for the island is simply unfavoured. Advisers and helpers from the Peninsula, in agriculture for example, are treated with derision : the islanders *know* there is nothing practical to be done. Only, the Church persuades them, to pray. And so the Mass and also goats' horns— as will be described in a later section on religion and witchcraft —are often thought more directly efficacious than tree planting and improved agricultural methods.

DEPOPULATION OR REORIENTATION

The only alternative to staying and sitting out the *año ruin* has always been seen as emigration. The latter is now accelerating as a result of increasing contact with the north, for this has led to a rise in the number and standard of material wants. The old land will not yield any more than before and so, with all the possible advantages and disadvantages, the people leave it. Sometimes they go to help farm more viable land belonging to a relative, but more usually they become either *medianeros* or else wage-earners.

The *medianero* works a richer man's land in exchange for a half share in the profits. At its worst, half the produce of a dozen plots goes to an absent owner, the other half just keeping alive the dozen families who work them. At its best, as in the new Fuerteventura tomato plantations, the plot is large, the gear modern, the work interesting, the return for the labour locally good.

But to many there is no alternative to becoming wage-earners in urban areas, not merely in Gran Canaria and Spain but in all the parts of Europe and America where the Spanish worker can go. Many of them will be unhappy, unsuited by their upbringing to the different environment. Few on Fuerteventura have any idea of what life in a big city means. For those who know how to choose, and are strong-minded enough to do so, it would mean education, sufficient well-balanced food and more carefully controlled health, and a broader way of life in all sorts of ways. For others it would mean greater cravings, due to social-cum-advertising pressures, increased sexual stimulus and so on; and overcrowding, bad air, incessant noise and adulterated food;

and mass reading matter and passive entertainment and the rest. The older people may appreciate this, the young ones certainly do not.

Only a mixture of pessimism, lack of training and absence of capital prevents the islanders from making a living at national standards without leaving Fuerteventura. At present they alternate between blaming the government for not giving them more financial and technical aid and carrying the statue of the Virgin shoulder-high because it has rained. But, inexorably, the water shortage will get worse. Spanish Sahara, the island's *memento mori* only fifty sea-miles away, supports at a lower level still a population the size of Fuerteventura's on an area about one hundred and fifty times larger. In insisting upon dependence on northern-type agriculture, the country people are simply being unrealistic.

Apart from fishing, and of course tourism, an obvious reorientation is towards small industries. These would supply island needs and also yield exports and goods for sale to the tourists. The primary materials already produced by the island are wool and hides, plant fibres, tomatoes and cochineal, and fish, but all are exported raw; some proportion just goes to waste on the island. The light industries could absorb all these. Spun wool, cloth and clothes; leather goods, like the shoe industry which gives a good living to many on the island of Menorca; ropes, mats, sacks; tomatoes are not exportable which are too big or too small for northern tastes or are already reddening or have the least external blemish, and a factory could be set up to can these, since they are visibly much in excess of the islanders' consumption; the raw cochineal could be turned locally into the non-poisonous colouring powder used by food and cosmetic makers; an improved fishing fleet could supply a fish-canning factory. Boat-building and furniture-making are possibilities, absorbing, as would many of the light industries proposed, most of the island's craftsmen and apprentices. It will be shown later that, as everywhere, craftwork has little chance of survival in the island, for only the carpenters, going over to working on the new build-

142

Page 143: (right) Saddle-maker at Casillas del Angel. He was the last leather worker; (below) Fishermen at Pozo Negro. The man on the left has 'Mechta-Afalou' features.

Page 144: (above) Maria Cerdeña, the island's last potter, with a *tofio* or milking pot. Note her 'Mechta-Afalou' face; (below) Jacinto Cerdeña and his wife, basketry-workers

ing sites, are not being affected by the influx of cheaper, and usually poorer, machine-made goods. Also, Fuerteventura's soil is a natural resource : as in the island of Ibiza, a small enterprise could be started for making roof and floor tiles and cheap machine-made earthenware pottery. A small quantity of salt is produced, but exploitations by large-scale pans—on an island which nature has endowed with little but sea-water and heat—would provide many with work. More grandiosely, a factory to make the cement which Spain so much needs is possible, experts having declared the rocks suitable.

But it is no good suggesting schemes which need much capital, since at the moment it is only readily available, from state or individual sources, for the development of tourist resorts, from which the average shepherd or farmer does not benefit; many are even suffering. As an example of the schemes which, at present, seem bound to be stillborn for lack of capital, here is a summary of the breathtaking 'Plan Chamorro', published by a captain of that name, a member of the Civil Guard. Fuerteventura and Lanzarote are to be treated as one. Energy is to be provided partly by harnessing the Montaña del Fuego, a Lanzarote volcano where a stick thrust into a hole in the ground bursts into flames in a few minutes, and partly, taking advantage of the trade winds, by immense wind-driven generators. Seawater will be distilled; this was also optimistically called for by the general workers' conference. Fish offal will provide the raw materials for factories producing oils and glues, fish-skin leather goods, photographic emulsion, flans, fish wool, fish-foam noise insulator and, with suitable additives, margarine and glycerine, varnish and paint, and soap. Cultivations of cotton, flax, ramie, jute and agave, together with thuya and esparto, the last two needing acclimatising first, will yield cellulose which, in turn, can be made into artificial silk like rayon, and even into artificial wool. Cardboard will be produced from the leaves and trunks of the banana trees of the other islands. To cut out inter-island transport troubles, Lanzarote and Fuerteventura would be linked, via Isla Lobos, by an underground railway.

I

FUERTEVENTURA

It might not take much to stem the emigration of the country people of Fuerteventura. Most dislike travel and, if possible, often return to the island as soon as they hear that it has rained, for they are happiest in their own villages. Recently, in Antigua, somebody won an advertising campaign's fortnight's holiday for two in Málaga . . . neither the winner nor anybody else could be persuaded to take it, and the prize went unused.

10   ISLAND WORK

OUTLINING the main occupations affords an oppor-
tunity to introduce some of the descendants of all the
early immigrants and influences. The first three occupations cover the bulk of the continuing ancient livelihoods; the
latter trio have either almost ended or, like those of the potter and
also of a Casillas del Angel saddle-maker, have just been given
up. In fact, the society in which these occupations played essential parts is rapidly disappearing and will be a matter of history
in a few years' time.

A farm already ancient, the cobbled courtyard with many doors
around it. An old tree droops near the centre, a young palm
grows in a corner. Reached up a short wooden staircase, a carved
balcony, made for leisure, fronts the earth-roofed upper storey.
In the bedroom a four-poster bed with lace hangings, coarse
woollen blankets and, resting on springing of plaited palm, a straw
mattress. Between the bed and a wooden chest there is a heavy
palm mat. The huge iron-bound box holds clothes, a bible and
a few letters. Long skirts, a white blouse, a broad-brimmed straw
hat—or, if it were Sunday, a blue silk one in the Andalucian
style—and the woman of the house was ready for the day. On
her feet she has flat kid-skin shoes, short-lived like those of gannet-
skin once worn by women in the Outer Hebrides. The farmer's
wife's kitchen is dark and sooty, especially the great hod-shaped
smoke-catcher above the stone counter on which stands the little
cooking hearths. Heavy red earthenware pots and dishes run the

147

length of the stone bench which is built against the wall opposite the hearths. A huge stone mortar for crushing up maize stands on the floor in a corner, a long powerful pounder resting in its deep bowl. In another corner, on the stone counter, there is a rotary hand-mill for grinding wheat and barley. Hanging up out of the way of the rats, a goat-skin for making butter, another holding flour. Below, the cheese-making stool. A block of black ashy barilla, the soap in common use, and an earthenware bowl. Here and there wooden wine jars, a palm broom, a little saffron-stained mortar, the long, metal-tipped pole used in barilla-making. A man comes and borrows one of the grain-measures, a heap of wooden boxes. In the courtyard there are men saddling the donkeys and the camel, preparing the oxen for ploughing, filling sacks with grain to take into the village. In the sooty kitchen the twig fire crackles into flame, the day has begun.

A FARMING FAMILY

The Brito's farm is perhaps the highest inhabited dwelling in the island. Lying halfway betwen Betancuria and Santa Inés, the whitewashed building runs along a terrace within a hidden bowl; the latter is the source of a long, deep gorge, Barranco de la Peña. Primitiva Brito, in a brown smock with frilly pyjamas showing about the ankle, and a faded straw hat, is hard to spot as, amongst the dusty yellow stones and grey bushes of the sienna-washed *barranco*, she goes about her routine of collecting herbs, twigs and goat fodder; she is small, thin and wiry, with a tanned, wrinkled face. Francisco Brito is an ordinary farmer. Now eighty, his face, brown and stubbled like a harvested cornfield, sets in a rather blank expression, but he becomes perceptive and smiling when he speaks; blunt in conversation and generous in action, he accepts his life, hoping only for rain for his land. He is helped by his son Lorentiano, the last of eight children to be at home. And Lorentiano, at forty around the upper end of the age group now seeking to break with traditional island life, is in turn helped by a lean grey dog.

148

A visitor to the farmhouse shares the family meal at a small table with benches, all of green-painted wood. A midday meal would often consist of a plate of boiled peeled potatoes, a dish of dried figs, a heap of spring onions, a little bowl of oil and—the centre piece—a huge basin of dampened *gofio*. Each person begins by plunging a hand into the *gofio*, taking enough to knead up a modest ball.

Gofio is another legacy of the pre-conquest islanders, a way of preparing and eating grain, and it is still the basic ingredient of most meals of the common people. Nowadays it may be made of wheat, maize, barley, chick peas, carob beans, almost any grain at all, usually a mixture of two or three, with a preference in the above order. The seeds of wild plants are sometimes used too, the hungry people having a wide knowledge of natural foods. Apart, for example, from the seeds of the wild vetch-like *cuchihuela* (*Carrichtera annua*) and the pith of the milk-thistle *cardo corona* (*Silybum marianum*), the islanders have turned during famines to the seeds of the glassworts, *cosco* and *barilla*. The pods only open in damp conditions, and one method employed is to tip them into pools and trample on them; the seed lies at the bottom and is recouped when the pool is emptied. Probably for lack of fresh water, sea water is used, so that the resulting chocolate-coloured flour is very salty. Luis Diego Cuscoy, who noted the method just described in use in Tenerife in 1941, calculated that four people could obtain a bushel of seed for a week's work. The rigours of the Civil War obviously did not end in 1939. During earlier famine years, like 1770, a licence to burn the *cofe*, as the glassworts were then called, in order to extract the glass-making soda—the barilla of Europe—and sell it, was only granted against payment to the poor of its equal value in wheat, barley or money. To make *gofio*, the grain—from wheat to glasswort—is roasted in a broad shallow earthenware dish, then ground to a flour.

The *gofio* balls moulded, each person then dips them into the olive oil, and then eats them with a forked-up potato. Also, to start with, a few onions, and later the figs. The figs, as one often heard, are very small, and Sr Brito does not know why. On the island of Hierro, inheritance interferes with pruning : a poor person may leave only a fig tree . . . a branch to each child. On Fuerteventura it is just not the custom to prune, probably for fear of reducing the immediate crop. The meal draws to an end. There is no cheese nor milk or water. To finish, there is black coffee and a plate of *pan biscochado*, literally 'biscuited bread', stale broken-up loaves baked hard.

Francisco Brito enjoys showing the rare visitor around his farm. He has 50 sheep, the lambs most of the time with carved wooden bits in their mouths to prevent them sucking, and still uses the Mahoh *tofio* milking pot; this is an open, round earthenware vessel with a broad jutting spout. Field irrigation is by the typical Arab *noria*, the water-raising animal-driven wheel to be seen in eastern Spain : Paco Brito made his own, and powers it by harnessing his camel or one of the donkeys to it. The farm has many mature fruit trees, a vast cactus clump which shelters the latrine, and field-crops ranging from wheat to fodder saffron.

The camel, which pulls the Roman plough in a long-established yoking with a donkey, is usually tethered behind the house. It makes a hostile whistling noise through its nose on being approached. The farmer displays it as one does a thoroughbred, with a warning to keep clear : it is a male and vicious because it is the mating season. The camel was worth twelve thousand pesetas or so until not long ago, but now that the Moroccans have opened their frontiers they can be bought for half as much. Suddenly the camel puts out a tongue like a length of wet foam rubber and sets it and his flabby lips into a sloppy rumbling vibration. There used to be far more camels, but they are being replaced by tractors. A Moor from Cape Juby used to sell twenty or thirty young ones on Fuerteventura every year, but the last time he came he did not sell any and so has not been since. The first camels were probably captured on the adjacent continent in the fifteenth century, and would soon have been at home on the arid plains of Fuerteventura. At the beginning of the twentieth century the camel population had reached 6,000; about then a German agent had to be prevented from buying them all up for use in the war against the Bantu Hereros. Not merely suited climatically to Fuerteventura, the camel's attraction to the islanders lies in its strength, for they maintain that, balanced on the W-shaped saddles of tamarisk wood, loads of up to 500kg are possible.

From the threshing pan on which the camel is tethered there is a chute direct into a straw room below, at the back of the stable, itself entered from the next terrace down. Such organisation is rare. A dying custom is that of storing grain in hollow hay-stacks. The pre-conquest people are recorded as having used a hollow cairn, or *taro*, for hanging meat to dry and generally storing provisions; from St Kilda to central Africa there are parallels. The word *taro*, recalled in the name of the highest point of the eastern cordillera, Rosa del Taro, 593m—perhaps here a summit cairn—is now meaningless to the islanders.

A less-easily superseded Mahoh legacy was the rotary quern, for grinding grain. But the Britos now use theirs only for cracking up maize for the animals, their other grain going to the centrally-placed power mill. Generally similar to those used in Scotland until recently, and still current in many parts of the world, Fuerteventura's hand querns were, at their most evolved, driven by an overhead crank with its upper end in a socket in the ceiling; they were of grey lava, with the Mahohs favouring a goat bone as a pivot. A few huge camel-driven querns, *tahonas*, are still in use in the north, at Los Lajares; this village gets its name from a slabby lava-field just to its south, the island's quern quarry.

About to leave the Britos' farm, the visitor's eye may be caught by a glinting trickle of water which, seeping out of the ground beside the farmhouse, is collected in a small trough for drinking and then overflows into a huge one which is used for clothes washing. It was this trickle which showed Francisco Brito that they could live in the bowl and so led him to settle and build. It is a rare experience to find somebody who is satisfied with his work—who, in seemingly wanting a witness to it, is, not least, wanting somebody else to get some satisfaction from it too. Emigrating when a young man to Buenos Aires, he came back. The bowl was then barren uninhabited hillside.

A SHEPHERD

Every day, somewhere in one of the Antigua-facing ravines of the western cordillera, a short strongly built man in a rotting brown hat can be seen, hunched and motionless, staring gloomily at a straggle of goats and sheep. At a distance there is not a plant nor a blade of grass anywhere, and the flock appears only to be making a pretence of grazing, perhaps from habit.

On a spine in the middle of Salvador Santana's territory stands the two-roomed shack which is his working base. Only the flock is actually his, the few terraces below he works—if it rains—on the usual half-profits agreement. The scene is typical : the decaying farm, the owner absent, perhaps no longer even residing on the island, a *medianero* who lives in the nearest village.

Salvador's regular income stems from a two-kilo cheese he makes each afternoon. About midday the flock is driven back to the shack, to an incessant, musical encouragement: *'Jaira—jaira—jaira—jaira'*, the Mahoh word for goat. Or, severely : *'Cabra! Por a-quíííí!'* Especially the last long-drawn-out syllable. 'Goat! Come over here!' The animal pen, cut back into the rock, shares a wall with the shack. The sheep are medium-sized, all ewes and hornless, and have long faces with ears which lie out horizontally; the rams of the breed have curly horns, as do, for example, the Highland Blackface. Some of the goats are soon balancing on blocks of stone in the middle of the pen, one gets up onto the roof of the shack; of every imaginable pattern of black and white, brown and grey, some with a stripe of colour along the back, the nannies have short horns which grow backwards and curve slightly downwards, but with the abruptly narrowing tip often curling up again; Salvador's one billy goat has horns which, though straight overall, grow in a screw, each splaying out at about forty-five degrees to his backbone. All the goats have very

152

short coats, except for a surprisingly hairy and rather degenerate-looking specimen, which Salvador says occasionally turns up.

Two long-faced donkeys, tied to each other by a length of rope, have tangled themselves up with the olive tree. There are cats and hens scuttling about, a puppy squeaking from a stable at the further side of the house, and fish in the open-air water cistern. Inside one is greeted from below a wigwam of sticks in the corner by the bleating of a kid.

Salvador sits on some white sacks bearing in Spanish, many times repeated, the words : 'Gift of the People of the United States of America'. Above the shepherd's head a calendar with the Virgin of Fatima on it has a list of prayer injunctions and three aims : 'Salvation, Peace, and the Conversion of Russia'.

Salvador opens the demonstration with :

> *'Para hacer queso*
> *Sal y peso.'*
> 'Cheese is made
> With salt and strength.'

In the middle of the dusty floor stands a tall narrow yellow tin, the olive-oil can which has so many uses in Spain and, in Salvador's work, has replaced a goat-skin. This one holds about ten litres of curdled milk, sheep's and goat's mixed, this morning's. Salvador plunges his hairy brown arm in up above the elbow to see if it is ready. Muttering encouragement to the invisible curds at the bottom, he churns them about with his hand. At length he pulls up a sloppy blob and pronounces it done.

Salvador next chooses one of a heap of long flat strips of plaited palm and coils it up until he has a circular centre space, in which the cheese will be made, of about twenty centimetres diameter. He puts it on the cheese stool, which has a pattern sunk into its face, the one schoolboys always make with their compasses, a sort of star. Amongst the ruins of a village with both Mahoh and post-conquest occupation—on the east coast El Esquen spine—there is a carefully-shaped, runnelled slab of lava, probably an early version of the same stool. Salvador's stool also bears, in raised, back-to-front metal letters, 'A 43', his Antigua

153

Co-operative number. The shepherd says people used to put any-thing in before, for example, potatoes, stones, rags, though it was not always the shepherd's work, often the girl who was making the cheese used to eat so much she had to make up for it some-how. He puts the plaited circle on the stool and begins filling it with handfuls of curds which he is hauling out of the depths of the can. The kid has escaped from its pen and, obviously frantic with hunger, races about trying to find the source of the milk, sucking at the dripping legs of the cheese stool, almost knocking over the whey can. The shepherd explains that its parent nanny did not want it and it is not worth looking after specially as the year is too far on; it will have to be killed. Salvador always sum-marises the gloomy topics with a sighing : *'Sí, Señor. . . .'*

He plops the last wad of white rubbery curds onto the embryo cheese, and starts the *peso* part : pressing out the remaining whey. This drips off the runnelled stool into a rusty tin, to be eventually fed back to the animals. The cheese starts to shine, it is done. Next one side is plastered with crude white salt crystals. That night the other side will be salted, the following morning the cheese will go up on the platform of the watermill, to dry out for a day or two in the wind.

When eight days old it is ready, by agreement, for sale to the Antigua Co-operative. Salvador received, in the late 1960s, 72 pesetas a kilo. The local shops sell it at 80 a kilo, and although imported Dutch processed cheese is at 50, many locals think it disgusting stuff. Salvador adds that much of the island cheese is sold in Las Palmas, at 120 a kilo or over.

There are all sorts of variations in agreements and income sources among the island shepherds; Salvador's livelihood is as typical as any. At present his flock is about twenty strong. The thirteen adult milkers and the billy goat are worth about 1,000 pesetas each but, as it is going to be a hard summer again for grazing, their value will gradually drop to half, to that of mere meat; the rest of the animals are lambs and kids of various ages, at present worth from 100 at a month old to the 1,000 at maturity. Salvador's capital, then, is almost 20,000, but, if the drought forces him to sell—rather than watch the animals starve, thus giving no milk and some even dying—he will find that, when it rains and he wants to renew the flock out of any money still remaining to him, prices will be back to normal, to twice the amount for which he had to sell. The shepherd says gloomily that then he would have to find other work.

The meat market is of course always better outside the money-lacking island, but Cabildo policy has long been not to allow animals to be exported in times of drought : apart from reducing the island's food supplies, the flocks can often not be re-established. If shipping is permitted it is only against a high deposit returnable when a similar animal comes back in. It is not clear, of course, what else the people can do but sell and spend the money if there is no grazing to be turned into marketable cheese; but such is the law. The present flock clearances caused by the land speculators are an embarrassment to the Cabildo, but tourism always comes first. Generally, to get animals out in spite of the ban, usually to '*algun moro*' in Africa, it is customary to slaughter them and ship the carcasses out as 'fish'.

His income, by local standards, is not too bad; but it depends, of course, on whether he can find the grazing. His thirteen milking sheep and goats give about 12 litres of milk a day which yield 2 kilos of cheese for sale and a quarter-kilo one for himself; sales thus bring in 144 pesetas. Less the $6\frac{1}{2}$ kilos of maize fed to the milkers daily to make up for the chronically bad grazing; this costs about 35 pesetas a day. The grazing around the old farmhouse is thrown into the *medianero* contract, but Salvador has to rent far more from other people in order to get enough for his small flock : the animals pasture the first few ridges and ravines northwards, which cost him 3,000 pesetas for a year's rent, say 8 pesetas a day. So net cheese income is about 100 pesetas a day, a fifth above the minimum legal hire for a man . . . but, according to a government study of June 1967, *only half the national average*. In addition, apart from the daily small cheese and the negligible meat and skins, the fleeces bring in a little each spring : there are at present eight sheep and they

155

give 2 kilos of greasy wool each at about 20 pesetas a kilo, a total of 320 more. An equal amount might be his half-share of the crop off the two olive trees and the three carobs. Of the islanders' reputedly huge incomes from crops in the occasional rainy year, one dares not ask : the winter's drought has scorched up every terrace Salvador has sowed, and he has had to decide to let the animals finish off the dwarfish yellow-tinged barley shoots.

A single man, he is not badly off. Neither is his friend Juanito, who looks after somebody else's flock for 1,000 a week; he is married and has two children. But Salvador's sister and her husband, with whom he lives, have five children, some people have ten, and usually their income is no more than Salvador's, unless, as is often the case, both husband and wife earn. Salvador's work is light and easy. Further, he says he likes being up on the mountain, and wouldn't want to be anywhere else, although, as he says, the days are long up there, just himself and the goats.

Two communal events, which must have added greatly to a shepherd's life, were the *majadilla* and the *gambuesa*, the latter still held. It is only in the most remote regions that one comes across the remains of the *majadillas*, places where shepherds and their flocks, forced to the inhospitable areas in search of pasture, used to gather to pass the night together. One abandonel *majadilla* high in the eastern cordillera consists of a wall enclosing the flattish summit of a mound; built into the wall, like sentry boxes, are several one-room ruins. The centre of the enclosure is whitened by the inevitable limpet shells, amongst them sherds of rough red recent pottery, including a fragment made into a spindle whorl. One imagines the long staves whacking the unruly animals into the big pen, and, in the gloom, some of the shepherds milking and others getting a fire going, and then them all sitting down against a sheltered wall and stuffing themselves with *gofio* balls and limpets.

The *gambuesa*, also held in the centre of isolated regions, differs in that it is a monthly communal round-up of free-roaming animals, needing only a large corral. One regular *gambuesa* is held at Fuente de las Ovejas, Sheep Spring, in the eastern cordillera Barranco de la Torre. Sunk in a hidden, overhung channel in the 2km-wide bed of the gorge, the corral loses its silent unfrequented air once a month.

An oldish brown-faced man with a staff arrives from up the *barranco*, a dog at his heels. At the same time there is a whistle from the mountain sky-line, and a figure with an immense pole in its hand appears. As if they have been waiting for the signal, the silhouette of Little Falcon Mountain—the *barranco*'s southern wall—begins to ripple as ten or fifteen flocks appear and spread out against the dusty sky. These animals are running, for they live in a wild state and are not used to shepherds, and so it is more of a hunt than a simple driving-in of flocks. The men are shouting and swearing, flinging themselves desperately down the almost vertical mountainside with the aid of the long staffs. The sheep and goats have recognised the corral below and those coming from the left attempt to leave the scene to the right, streaming away in twos and threes. The dogs are useless. Lobbing small boulders to turn the animals off, some of the shepherds cross above and, by running and vaulting, get ahead and send them down again. Very soon, in all only a matter of a few minutes, the animals are massed before the creep into the corral, and are ducking through one by one.

All penned inside, the shepherds jump up onto the wall and draw breath. There are fourteen of them, including two boys and several old fellows; they wear shirts, trousers and a variety of hats, and either cracked leather boots or the popular cheap white canvas shoes with black rubber soles. One old man is girt with a cummerbund. Salvador's brother-in-law, who is tall and has blue eyes and fair skin, is there, and his son, and Gregorio who works a tomato patch up the *barranco*.

Like most Canary shepherds, they each carry a very long staff. But these, which have iron-spiked tips, are not merely a local version of the crook : they are for vaulting. Here is another of the Mahohs' legacies, though their poles were tipped with goat horns. The lance-like staffs, originally called something like *tezeres*, up to two and a half metres long, are used for fast descents of the steep loose mountain slopes. This enables the shepherds to control and keep up with the goats without limiting their pasturage, since only by letting the animals cover an immense area each day can they find enough to eat. This, incidentally, is why there are no walls, and a man has to spend his time watching over a few animals; but then, like the way the poor endlessly divide their already limited agricultural land into minute, uneconomic plots, this is Spain. To get back to the vaulting staffs, the real mountain-dwellers of Fuerteventura, though now few, rarely go out without their poles, goats or not, since they are as accustomed to use them to swing down the ravine walls as a one-legged man to his crutch.

The oldest shepherd, short and square-faced, is the one who is in charge of this area and its *gambuesas*. This part of the coast, not yet having been sold by the *ayuntamiento*, or local council, to the land speculation companies, unlike great parts, is still common grazing land. Any parishioner who wishes can turn his sheep or goats loose onto it. Salvador, for example, has had eight goats there for several months, to spare the grazing on his personal territory.

The word always used for a free-roaming animal is *guanil* and, like *gambuesa*, it was used by the Mahohs in the same sense. In addition to chanting the Mahoh name for goat to keep the flocks moving, *jaira-jaira-jaira*, the shepherds use the pre-conquest word *baifo*, a kid or lamb, more readily than the Castilian equivalents.

At length the men start work on the animals. New lambs and kids are ear-marked; some adults are singled out, to go back with their owners for shearing or milking, or eating; the testicles are slashed off a shrieking billy goat, which is then allowed to career away down the *barranco*. Several of the shepherds have brought food—brown-chequered woven bags are common—and they eat as the work permits.

The last batch of goats is dealt with, just as peseta-size splodges of warm rain spatter the dust. They all gather up their bags, the selected animals are pushed outside. A pause to separate the dogs, for a yellow whippety creature, one of those like the Ibiza hounds, has attacked a member of the ancient grey-and-gold race. Then the shepherds troop off across the plain, the animals under control, outnumbered by men and sticks. One shepherd has somehow killed a couple of grey and white rabbits. Somebody remarks, regretfully, that there used once to be many more shepherds at the *gambuesas*.

FISHERMEN

At Cotillo everyone is 'going down to the beach', the words are heard on all sides. Yesterday, 3 April, was the opening of the year's fishing, summer and a calm sea at last. The excitement of the first catches is in the air. Juan Hierro, the tall, thin, bespectacled north-end buyer, asks how many boats are out, and is told five have been away since early morning. His van lurches past an enormous *nasa* cage-trap and down a ramp onto the shingle. The bay is a good one for small boats, perhaps a hundred metres long and very narrow, with a low island-cum-reef blocking the attack of the breakers; the water looks deep. The arms of the bay, black rocks, are high, with shacks built out along them. The first of the fishing boats is just chugging into sight round the southern promontory. It reaches the shore and the two short stocky fishermen jump out into the shallows and pull the craft, typically double-bowed and perhaps made by Cotillo's boat-builder, up to the shingle edge. Soon a centipede-like line, tugging and shouting, its many feet digging into the stones, is struggling up the beach, the launch reluctantly following, one of the crew placing and replacing the rollers. 'She's ours!' somebody shouts as they go over the tide-ridge, but they drag on until the boat's well clear.

The catch is lying on the floorboards, mainly a couple of hundred little cigar-shaped *cabrillos*, a type of sea-perch, cream and brown mottled. There are also a few silver-blue bream, a couple of ferocious and powerful dentex, a slender olive-brown meagre, a hideous red warty scorpion-fish with brown freckles.

159

One of the fishermen, using a basket, gets them out onto a strip of canvas in the shelter of the boat, and now it is the turn of the fish-mistress, a fat no-nonsense woman swaddled in brown. The housewives of Cotillo crowd round. As far as one can tell, the fish-mistress allots them to what she feels like. She uses a crude balance, and as weights has a couple of beach stones, presumably locally approved, which she treats as a kilo each. She deals summarily with the women, who take their lots and go off to scale them at the edge of the sea. The fish-mistress sells about six kilos. Then it is Juan Hierro's turn, and he automatically takes the rest, about 40 kilos. He pays on the spot, the same price as the locals, 15 to 20 pesetas a kilo. The *cabrillos*, for example, will resell at 30 pesetas a kilo in the port, or get exported to Grand Canary.

The two fishermen have done well, taking about 800 pesetas, or £5, for the day's line fishing. Out of this comes tackle, fuel and boat maintenance. And of course they can only fish from April to September at the outside, having to find other work for half the year. Many of the village's fishermen are still working in the tomatoes in the south, but they are expected soon. Then some forty boats will stretch the length of the beach.

The idea of fresh-water fishing would probably bring an incredulous smile to the face of an islander. Even more fantastic must seem the use to which will be put several immense concrete reservoirs being built on an arid plain near the south-western settlement of Las Hermosas : a German is to breed fresh-water fish in them. A foreign technician will be arriving soon. The islander in charge is very pleased with his job. The fish will be bred there and exported to Europe in polythene bags. Local demand for inedible fish will, of course, be negligible, whilst local difficulties—lack of fresh water and the distance the fish must travel and arrive alive—one would have thought daunting, and economically hopeless. Breeding camels in Great Britain, for export to Africa, could scarcely be harder. Still, it will employ several men. Colocynth cultivation may not be the only possible boom.

160

THE LAST POTTER

As in many primitive communities, Fuerteventura's pottery-making was always women's work. At Chipude, in Gomera, the last craftswomen now work for tourism, asking exorbitant prices for the heavy coarse pots, and five *duros* for permission to take their photographs. This was one alternative to extinction. In Fuerteventura, and covering all crafts, co-operative shops would be a preferable course.

From the door of her Santa Inés workshop, María Dolores Cerdeña, Fuerteventura's last potter, now retired, points up a *barranco* opposite : the only place for getting the earth, in the entire island apparently, is at Majuelo. The burnt yellow slope of the ravine is pitted with shallow holes. There is nothing unusual in the potter's technique. The vessel is shaped by hand from a lump of earth, without a wheel; the main tools are a hollow-edged scrap of iron for the convexities and two or three small pieces of hard, sharp-edged wood for the concavities. Formed, the pot is then allowed to dry for a day or two. On the ground outside is a spread of ash on which stand four small stones in a line : the unfired pots are next arranged upon these and covered with wood, which is lit, a typical 'bonfire kiln'. Once fired, the pots are burnished with a series of water-worn pebbles, the finest of which come from a beach renowned for such smooth and glossy stones; they look like fine-grained basalt. The pot is always a rich red-brown, decorated with the black smudges and bars caused by the burning out of the twigs which have actually touched it during firing. The shapes are simple and elegant, any handles or lips being a part of the body and not stuck on. The Santa Inés potter seems never to have decorated her pots, nor in the island does one see a recent one with decoration. The largest is the water-carrier, or *bernegal* : the sides bulge far outwards, base and mouth being less than half the width, like a huge squat children's top. She also made *tofios*, the milking pots, and recalls Paco Brito's; one she has left would be 17 *duros*, 50 new pence.

The Mahohs are thought to have got their earth from up at

Majuelo too, 'just as we Christians have done since'. The primitive work is said to have been better than the modern. These sharp distinctions between 'them' and 'us' are often heard. But both the potter's squat *tofio* pot and square powerful face have in fact come down from the Mahohs.

The *tofio* has proved the longest-lived of all the pre-conquest pottery. However, the author saw hardly any pots which had been made during the last few hundred years, and other forms may have survived until recently too. For example, the waterpot is certainly called a *bernegal*, a word in use in peninsular Spain and South America too, but this does not mean that the shape could not be descended from a pre-conquest vessel—but such details are studies in themselves. The *tofio* kept going, first, because pottery-making was every woman's work and Mahoh women survived the conquest; and, second, because, although the dominant European class would have wanted finer crockery than the bulk of the Mahoh ware—a want which of course gradually spread to the common people to the present extreme of ending local pottery—the *tofio* would always have done for milking. Naturally, the Castilians would not have stooped to pot-making, nor would it have been worthwhile sending to Europe for a pot so often broken; in the same way the water-carrier may have long survived. The pre-conquest *tofios* often bore incised festoons and other exuberant decorations, long discarded for many possible reasons : prejudice by the settler class, the potters' need to hide their ancestry, the customary degeneration of a slowly dying craft.

As for the potter's square jaw, descended from one of the two main Mahoh physical types, the 'Mechta-Afalou', it is a part of the evidence that a number of islanders survived the fighting, no doubt mainly women. By analogy with the better documented main islands, those who did not actually marry their conquerors would have hastened to take on European names, for the sake of their children, Mahoh or half-caste : after the fall of Tenerife and Gran Canaria towards the end of the century, most men changed their name to Fernando and most women to Isabel, in homage to their Peninsula monarchs. But physical features are less simply altered, and the Mahoh woman and her milking pot have managed in some measure to reach the present day, though neither are easy to find.

BASKETMAKERS

At first Jacinto Cerdeña, also of Santa Inés, has been rather miserable, he keeps saying he is too ill to work. But, pulling out his baskets and talking about them, and in front of enthusiasm for his work, he cheers up, and insists on bringing out every single one, and on sending his wife to find others in use in the house.

The baskets are almost entirely made of palm, with a little bamboo in the very large ones where the mood has taken him. Perhaps 80cm deep, and as broad at the mouth, the big baskets taper slightly to a square base. The frame, which is to say the base and the side verticals, is made from the spine of the palm frond, split with a knife into long, strong strips; the walls of the basket are then made by weaving in the remaining part of the frond, the pointed flexible ribs, of which each mature frond has many dozen. The role of the latter is sometimes played by the bamboo, split into thin strips. In one huge basket the bamboo is still green, and the few centimetres' width around the wall contrasts richly with the dry yellow of the palm. It takes about three days to make one of these big baskets, says Señor Cerdeña, and he receives 250 pesetas for each one. The demand is greater than he can supply; nevertheless he can think of only two other basket-makers on the island.

Apart from all sizes of rigid baskets, he makes three other palm-work, of splendidly fresh design. The first is the *cerrón*; Robert Louis Stevenson would have had much less trouble with Modestine if he had taken one of these Practical Donkey Loaders with him. Made in a soft flexible weave, it is simply two lengths of flat, strong palm-branchlet fabric, each about a metre and a half by three-quarters, joined to each other on three sides to make a long pouch. Filled fairly full of grain or potatoes, and

163

laid across the donkey, it sags to the shape of its back, forming itself into an even, hanging bag on each flank; it is comfortable for the animal and as stable as one can hope. The *portón* is a soft elastic container for things like salt. Made entirely from frond ribs, it is about 30cm wide at the mouth and twice as much at the base, so that it sits dumpily and will never fall over and spill its contents. Finally, Jacinto Cerdeña makes mats, immensely heavy and lasting. These consist of pleasingly broad strips of inter-laced frond ribs, the edges strongly bound though perhaps thus forming too much of a ridge.

But the basket-maker's wife also has a part. She makes the lightweight goods : hats and needlework baskets, for example. She describes the making of the hats. First the palm ribs are cut into centimetre-wide strips and then plaited together into a flat braid, using five or six strands at a time; she produces a made-up roll, of which there must thirty metres. This prepared, she goes on to make up the broad-brimmed 'straw' hat. Hers has the pecu-liarity that it looks like two hats stored one on top of the other, since it has a double brim; the under-brim has only a cloth crown. She agrees it all takes a very long time to make.

There is no sign of degeneracy, and one hopes that plastic containers will not abruptly replace the very fine island basket-work. But the Cerdeñas anyway see nobody likely to continue their craft, everybody is leaving Santa Inés.

A WEAVER

Juana García Cabrera lives near the village of Tiscamanita. Tall, middle-aged, she is optimistic over her craft and discusses it with-out reserve. Her standards are high, for she works to fill a com-munity need rather than for tourism.

A neighbour sells her the raw wool at 15 pesetas a kilo. She first washes and cards it; the cards are a speciality of El Aaiún, capital of the Ifni area of the Moroccan coast, opposite Lan-zarote, and until recently a Spanish enclave. Juana García next spins the wool herself, the few old women who still spin pro-

164

ducing very little, and for this uses a wooden spindle—its whorl at the very base—because the wheel has never reached Fuerteventura. Plying, rare, is on a heavier spindle.

Any dyeing is always done with bought chemicals; she has never used *orchilla* or *agicán* or other vegetables. The fleeces' natural colours, cream or brown, produce a check pattern popular in the island; for this reason the rare dark fleeces are valuable.

Her loom is the simplest four-shaft type, about 80cm in working width; the shuttle is boat-shaped. Her reeds, recalling the origin of the name, are of split reed, a huge species, said to now grow only near Pájara. Dentage is 3–6 warps to the centimetre. One cloth made by Juana García is a creamy twill, each bale some 9 *varas* or 8m long, wool being used for both warp and weft. A bale is often cut into three and the strips sewn into a near square, to make a 4–5 kilo blanket. Strong and durable, if rigid and napless to northern tastes, it is also sold for overcoats and jackets, and on the high cloud-damped pastures of the western islands a few shepherds still wear cloaks of this material.

But few can or will buy such good cloth nowadays, says Juana García. The emerging middle-class prefers inferior machine-made goods to the island blankets and pots, and the last craftsmen must hold on until the cycle of taste brings their richer countrymen back to their workshops. In the meantime, this weaver's main work is to make rag blankets. The hard-up islanders tear the rags into strips, buy the warp themselves—shoe-maker's thread at Tiscamanita—and deliver these to her. The blankets are rather over 2m each way, and for the two days' work she is paid 125 pesetas.

The Fuerteventura shepherd, when he goes off into the mountains with his flock, still takes his food in a *mochila*. The weaver points out a rather small one which she made to use up the end of a warp recently : it is a deepish flat bag made of wool, chequered brown and white, with bobbles around the seams and a long woollen cord to be slung over the shoulder. It is 40 pesetas. She also gets out an *alforja*, a woollen version of Jacinto Cerdeña's *cerrón* : a double bag for the donkey to carry. It is, in fact, a strip of the usual strong woollen cloth with a big deep *mochila* at each end, a mass of tassels and bright squares. A donkey could not wish for anything more decorative or more comfortable.

11   *CULTURE*

FUERTEVENTURA'S culture, here excluding occupations, can be divided between the traditional and the incoming European. At the time of writing, much of the traditional is still alive among the country people, but the inhabitants of the two ports live more or less in the European manner. On examination, the island's peculiar cultural characteristics are seen to have been acquired gradually, some at each of the various stages of its past.

LANGUAGE

Glas wrote in 1764 that the islanders 'neither speak nor understand any other language but Castilian, and this they pronounce most barbarously'. Castilian is of course the present tongue too. The common speech includes, however, a fair number of preconquest words, noted here and there already, the French-origin *jable* for sand wastes, and the names and corruptions already attributed to the enslaved Moors. Some words, like *papa* instead of *patata* for potato and the Cuban *gua-gua*, autobus, have come from the Spanish spoken in Central and South America. There is also a word or two of mysterious etymology, like *perenquén* for the gecko lizard. The rest is Castilian, including provincialisms, a few plain mistakes of probably very local extent, a number of more lasting corruptions and some unattractive pronunciation.

Provincialism can be illustrated by the preference of *millo*, perhaps brought by Galicians, to *maíz*, for maize. *Garrobero* is preferred to *algarrobo*, for the carob tree. Limitation of vocabu-

167

lary is shown, for example, by the fact that *cubo*, for bucket, is often not at all understood, the word *balde* being needed for comprehension.

Plain errors can be heard. *Herramienta*, tool, becomes *aramienta*, perhaps in confusion with *arar*, to plough. *Geranio*, geranium, as *genario*. *Encima*, above, familiar enough, can sound *encimba*. And the receptively-gendered abbreviation *una foto*, a photo, can be seen written *un afoto*, and is presumably thought of thus.

Torriani's 1590 map shows 'Guadalique' on the south-west coast, since become Agua Liques, which is rather more meaningful to the present islander as a name for the spring than a perhaps Moorish-origin name, which would derive from *wadi*. This corruption of incomprehensible names into more homely forms is common. The true aloe (*Aloë vera*), a garden plant and Castilian *zábila*, is sometimes *savia* or 'sap'; the squill *cebolla albarrana* can become *cebolla almorrana*, a 'piles' onion. As in the rest of the Canaries, the kestrel or *cernícalo* is often called a 'San Nicolas'. Needless to say, many cannot read or write, or only do so with difficulty.

As for general pronunciation, which Glas also compared 'to a man talking with something in his mouth', it varies, many of the country people being easy to understand, others less so. Lazy pronunciation often cuts off the last letter of a word. In the early post-conquest days, such Mahoh words as had stayed in use probably soon became permanently corrupted, as is suggested by the various forms of *efeguen*. Many of the present islanders are also guilty of the ugliest sound in Castilian, a common one on the Peninsula: a word like *cansado* loses its penultimate letter, its ending being hideously caterwauled. Hearing a couple of islanders holding a conversation across a valley, one is soon attuned to another characteristic sound, the excessively emphasised long dawn out last or penultimate syllable of each group of words: *'Que me falta una CAA-bra!' 'A donde va Us-TEEED?' 'Me voy p'a la mon-TAAA-ña!'* But the people are not nearly as hard to understand as are many regional pronunciations of the British Isles. Captain Glas may have been too severe, 'barbarously' is going too far.

Just below the Mahoh's fortress on the summit of Monte Cardón, on its coast-facing flank, a slight overhang at the base of a wall of black rock shelters a pure spring. The slithery descent towards it is thick with sherds, and one can be sure that the refuged islanders went down there to fill their water-pots. Nowadays the overhang holds four rough walls within which, having climbed a dusty track, islanders in their Sunday-best place lighted candles to the Virgen del Tanquito, the Virgin of the Little Cistern; they go there when in trouble to pray to be helped. It is said that the shape of the Virgin can be seen in the rock.

There are many ways of justifying the conquering of a people and the taking over of their country. Some have pointed to the 'advantages' which will accrue to the inhabitants, and later blame the bloodshed upon the 'non-co-operation' of the very people who are to benefit; others have claimed that 'racial superiority' on one side or 'heresy' on the other are justifiable reasons; yet others have produced ancient documents to prove that the land on which others live and work has really long been theirs; then there has always been the 'natural' right of expansion of a growing people, and their equally natural right to otherwise 'inadequately-exploited' resources; or, again, there is 'no alternative' but to conquer a 'potentially belligerent' country before it is strong enough to act. And so on. In the case of the Canary Islands the first justification was always given out; Viera y Clavijo has already been quoted. *'En esperance de les tourner et conuertir à la foy chrestienne'*, thus opens the chronicle of the conquest. In the hope of converting them to the Christian faith, the rationalization particularly fashionable in the fifteenth century, now out-of-date. No mention of the valuable slaves and dye-stuffs, of the goats and their products. Nor of the pleasure of conquering, being a hero, becoming powerful and rich, living off the work of others.

In 1404 Gadifer's priests wrote that the islanders were 'very firm in their faith. And it is very difficult to catch them alive; they are so strong that if one is trapped by the Christians and turns on them, they have no choice but to kill him'. Bontier and Le Verrier were responsible for organising the introduction of Catholicism into Fuerteventura. Hardly have the French a foothold than they write of the Mahohs, in the particularly untrustworthy Bethencourt chronicle : 'they are all Christians and bring their children as soon as they are born to the court of Baltharhais, and there they are baptised in a chapel which M. de Bethencourt has had built'. The priests would also have devoted their attention to the eradication of the pre-conquest places of worship : the need for stone to build the European settlers' houses could be satisfied from nowhere better.

For all this, in 1443 Gomes de Azurara, chronicler of the Portuguese expedition to Guinea, gave the island's Christian population as a mere eighty—the Mahohs were entrenched in the mountains, and in fact about that date came near to regaining the island. The Italian Alvise de Cadamosto, there about 1455, said there was no organised worship in the archipelago, some adored the sun, others the moon or stars, and there were as many as nine forms of 'idolatry'. It is recorded that, in Hierro, the islanders had to be broken of a preference for referring to Christ and the Virgin as Eraoranhan and Moreyba, the names of their proscribed deities. But, by the beginning of the seventeenth century, Tenerife's Guanche-extraction quarter is rioting because its privilege of carrying the Virgin's statue in the big annual procession is in jeopardy. Heathen practices had probably been eliminated throughout the Canaries, at least superficially.

Bethencourt's chapel lasted almost two centuries. Shortly before leaving the island for ever, at the end of 1405, he gave it 'an image of Our Lady, and some church robes and a really handsome missal and two little bells of a hundredweight each, and ordered that the chapel should be called Our Lady of Bethencourt'. Burnt down by pirates in 1593, it was rebuilt in the seventeenth century and is the present church of Betancuria. Of

170

impregnable aspect, with a square belfry tower roofed with tiles of many colours, the mature church is the dominant note in the ancient village. It contains a fresco showing a ship full of pie-faced men declaiming long texts which issue like ticker-tape from their mouths, a treatment of the conquerors of which Hieronymous Bosch would have approved, and, the subject of great reverence, the building also holds the fragments of the invaders' banner.

Bontier was a Franciscan and, in 1416, a group of men of this order, mainly Andalucians, arrived in Fuerteventura. Their head, Juan de Baeza, sounds to have been of the thin, gleaming line of worker-missionaries whose members include Bartolomé de las Casas and Albert Schweitzer. The Franciscans, of whom it is recorded, with emotion, that they carried the palm beams and tamarisk used in their convent on their own backs, wanted to teach the island people better agricultural methods, and Juan de Baeza was always writing to the Peninsula to try to get the necessary tools and a ship in which to visit the other islands. Unluckily there were then no international aid organisations, and his requests were not met. Worse, in the wake of the first invaders there was coming a stream of adventurers bent upon every form of pillage and profit. To be a foreigner was to be automatically hated; and the Franciscans were foreigners. One supposes that the group's initial zest for practical work petered out after the death of its leader. The friars certainly became gradually more and more parasitic upon the people until, unwanted, the whole order was suppressed as a result of the 1820 decree by the Cortes against the Spanish monasteries. 'The finest Gothic arch in the Canaries', as it has been described by the historian Serra Rafols, stands out against the sky in the roofless Convent of San Buenaventura; the mellow ruin is to be found a hundred metres up the water-course from Betancuria's church, on the eastern side of the *barranco*. It now holds only a few inscribed tomb-stones, and a couple of heaps of bones and skulls.

A third building, on the bank opposite the convent, suggests that religious saturation point in the tiny village must have

171

been reached by the seventeenth century. The size of an island church, the Hermitage of Diego of Alcalá was built about the cave where this Franciscan, head of the convent in the mid-fifteenth century, used to pray. Not far from a ruin, the floor is of drifted sand, the corners built up under centuries of bird-droppings. In a niche a damp and rickety San Diego, now patron saint of Spain, is staring at a length of rope on the wall above the cave—he is said to have used it on the Devil.

For the Devil was not absent on Fuerteventura and, in pursuit of his incarnate form, the Inquisition was soon present too. The Jews were expelled from Spain in 1492, and there is evidence that those of Fuerteventura received the attentions of the Holy Office. Renegade Moriscos, however, were the usual target; how Fuerteventura became overwhelmingly populated with Moors, and the consequences, has already been described. Witches were another form the Devil took, and in such quantity that, by 1757, the Inquisition was demanding that the Fuerteventura Cabildo should build a Witch-house, as a perpetual prison for enchant-resses and heretics. The Cabildo acknowledges that : 'The least of these islands is not unaware of the increasing number of people of both sexes who, forgetting God, give themselves up to the Devil by express or implicit alliance, and are proud to make their living from spells, fortune-telling, bewitchings and illegal healings, with injury to God and grave prejudice to their own souls and to those of others, and with menaces and false promises cheat the people, corrupt Christian customs, cause many to die and, worst of all, openly and without punishment flaunt their Diabolical profession'. It seems probable that the Penitence House was never built.

But, anyway, at the time of writing there are said to be only two or three cases left on the island. One, of the evil eye, is of a man whose potential mother-in-law disapproved of him : he did not marry the girl and has become more and more unwell. Another is of a potion which was accidentally drunk, at a *fiesta*, by the wrong man, who 'thereupon hung a bell around his own neck and went half the length of the island and back in the night';

in a community where goats are the obsession this sort of dementia could well occur, especially in an old person, as this man was. The La Oliva haunted house ends the list.

Religion is now much as on the Peninsula, of course. The village churches are simple mature buildings from which stem *romerías* to shrines, combinations of pilgrimage and picnic, and the water-processions and other religious functions. Minor devilry is still practised alongside : the agricultural adviser affirms, his tone of mixed resignation and disgust, that, to ensure a good crop, each fruit tree at the northern end of the island is hung with the horn of a male goat, and perhaps the Mahohs would have recognised these too.

EDUCATION

The island is remarkable for its new little schools. The people all agree how well the state is doing in education. 'My poor parents,' one hears, 'had no schooling at all.' And here the village is with a tall white building and a teacher. 'She lives in the upper part . . . and doesn't need to leave the house for a thing, neither water nor anything.' The secretary of the capital's *ayuntamiento* says that, in order to get teachers to the isolated parts of Spain, the government has been offering them up to a hundred per cent more than the basic national rate, according to the region. Thus Gran Canaria and Tenerife merited thirty per cent more and, the extreme supplement, Hierro and Fuerteventura teachers get a hundred per cent extra.

Making schools, like making roads, has also, of course, the advantage that it gives the rainless islanders work : national assistance without demoralisation. For this reason there are plenty of schools in Fuerteventura—each a combination of Primary and Secondary Modern, except for the one High School in the port—and the island can stand comparison with a few certainly no more remote islands of Great Britain, some of the Hebrides for example.

In the village of Antigua it is surprising to find no less than

173

three schools, strikingly new and unlike the rest of the houses. The outlying pair, in opposite directions, are only one and two kilometres respectively from the central school. However, as they only have four teachers between the three, and each school has to teach all age groups, the educational difficulties of the ancient one-teacher village school are still present. The younger children go only in the morning, the older ones in the afternoon. Yet total numbers are small enough to allow—were they all together— division into four classes according to age group, with the advantage of greater specialisation and of all-day school for each child, not to mention administrative economy in time and the wider facilities possible in a larger school.

The reason for Antigua's three schools is that, compared to northern children, the average Spanish child simply does not walk, nor do his parents expect him to do so. So he has to have his school near his home. This leads one to consider physical education and other outdoor activities. A 1967 Antigua school outing abandoned its walk to Betancuria halfway, the pupils being 'too tired' to go on, according to one girl. Apart from paramilitary youth outings, an unorganised kick-about with a football and the yearly walk to the local shrine, and unless he is put to work at any early age, the average child takes no more regular exercise than is imposed upon him by errands and going to school. There is no climate more agreeable than that of the Canaries, yet children or adults walking for pleasure are rarely met— though the country people of all ages have leisure—and rucksacks and tents are unusual possessions. 'What are you selling?' a country woman once asked the author as he heaved his pack along a high track in a remote part of Hierro. For that matter, everywhere in Spain the people wonder or even laugh at a figure with a rucksack, and that a woman should wear one is considered fantastic. Hunting seems the only reason for a walk into the countryside or up a mountain, at least for the average Spaniard. More, as everywhere else, so in Spain there is now a tendency towards being transported from place to place on wheels, or not going. But the wide education which results in an interest in

174

natural objects for their own sakes and not simply in order to exploit them, this standard of education is still lacking. Consequently there are few bird-spotters and botanists and climbers and fossil hunters and simply ramblers, and walking is just not fashionable. Too much walking 'ruins the feet'. Presumably both increasing urbanisation and better education will, in time, stimulate an interest in the countryside, and children will come to be encouraged to use their legs. In the meantime, the village of Antigua needs three separate new little schools.

Education of the adult country people is at present effectively impossible, due both to the lack of funds for classes and to the absence of transport to such evening courses as may be established. To these handicaps is allied the meagre or totally lacking natural lighting and electricity within the houses, which makes home study difficult or out of the question.

MEDICINE

The Mahohs believed in the value of goat butter and fat for curing ailments, simply anointing the afflicted part. The women used to bury butter in the ground; they considered that the longer the butter was cellared the more effective as a medicine it became. Of course, since the Mahoh form of worship included offerings of butter and milk, it is very probable that it was successful healing with ancient and rancid offerings—tried initially for their concentrate of the supernatural—which led to this practice of storing fats for medicine, with or without any trace of the original belief. Many Mahoh women seem to have been prevented from ever going back to their rancid but numenous unction, for quite a few pots of it have been found. Zeuner had a study of such Mahoh butter nearing publication at the time of his death. The latest butter-pot came to light on the outskirts of Antigua : a gigantic vessel, one of those almost a metre high, it stood in a round pit which was neatly lined with small stones.

Since the conquest and until very recently indeed, illnesses were treated by the *curanderos*. Their cures, some say, were

175

better and cheaper than the medical attention now available. The reader can judge from two examples of their prescriptions, one internal, the other external.

The little grey *yerba clin* (*Ajuga iva* var. *pseudo-iva*), a thyme much like a miniature pine, strong-smelling and rather furry, grows here and there on the hillside. Cases of *pulmonía*, a pain which locally takes one suddenly and, rather surprisingly, in the stomach, are very common. The victim of an attack searches at once for the plant—Paco Brito's wife has a supply dried ready—and chews a few leaves. If it doesn't taste bitter, it's a case of *pulmonía*. From being the doctor, the plant now becomes the medicine, for the stricken person must go on chewing its leaves until they do taste bitter. At this he stops, the medicine having pronounced itself sufficient—and is simultaneously cured. Though a specific for *pulmonía*, the plant is still much in use for any ailment. The Arabs use it to cure horses of epilepsy.

Doubtless *yerba clin* does have some action, which is more than one can say for the second of the old *curanderos'* remedies. A common prescription for a child born with a hernia was to take it to a quince tree on the day of the feast of St John the Baptist. A branch being split longways whilst still on the tree, the child was passed between the two lengths. The branch was then held together again, plastered thickly with mud and finally tied up with a cabbage leaf. If the branch, having been thus doctored, was found to live, then the child would recover from its disability.

Modern medicine is represented by doctors and chemists in each port, with a hospital in Puerto del Rosario, and by a doctor in Antigua. Many have to go to Gran Canaria for treatment since the hospital has only four beds; under-staffed, its patients' meals are brought into them by relatives. In a general store in the capital one can see spectacles tried on and bought like hats.

THE SUMMER SHACKS

Amanay is a typical west coast bay, black, precipitous, under perpetual pounding from great waves. And, in every possible gully and overhang, sheltering lean-to shanties and huts, all untenanted for most of the year.

These are the most striking human aspect of the west coast, and have always played an important part in the country people's lives. Apart from the frequent *gambuesas*, life at the summer shacks seems the only non-religious event of the year, and one can hardly doubt that it too is part of the Mahoh tradition. Simply, it is shellfish hunting during the low tides of the calm summer sea, and almost every sheltered bay, and certainly all near 'drinking water', have their *chozas*. The seasonal food-gatherers—men, women and children—leave their homes and travel, with animals and cooking pots and bedding, to their favourite bays, often a long way. There they live, beside the growing shell middens sometimes flecked with sherds of Mahoh pottery, and only go home once the best tides are past. One has but to look at the gigantic spread of mussel shells at the Junquillo and along the rest of the deserted zone to the north of Janey Barranco—too remote for the chicken-roughage seekers, who cart away all middens, old and new alike—to realise the length of time that the custom has been alive. The *chozas*, like those of the Mahohs, and many of them probably *are* Mahoh, are usually built into recesses in the cliffs, mere windbreaks for sleeping in. A few people make money out of the shellfish, drying them in the sun and then taking them into the villages for sale. The mussels are nowadays so rare that the collector has to go far into the sea, with a rope around his waist which a companion holds from the shore.

The empty shells, not written records, testify to the Mahohs' liking for limpets. History does however describe their four ways of catching fish : angling with hooks made of goat horn, poisoning rock pools with euphorbia juice, trapping with the aid of semi-circular rock walls which, at low tide, left fish stranded behind them, and, finally, a primitive form of the well known and Arab-originated *madrague*, current in the Mediterranean at present.

The Mahoh version of the *madrague* involved the use of nets made from palm and dragon. Some of the party, which included

177

the womenfolk, were beaters, wading through the water with clubs and driving the fish towards those who held the semi-circular nets at the ready. Presumably, as with the vastly larger-scale *madrague*, the nets were used in conjunction with natural features of the shore, the fish being eventually penned, rather than netted, for the Mahoh nets were perhaps too weak to take the strain of landing. The fish would probably be despatched in the shallow water with clubs. The Mahoh way of fishing has long been dead, boats and then current northern techniques probably taking over soon after the Europeans conquered the island. Still, one can imagine a Mahoh fishing party. Several families, perhaps with a common net, and all good swimmers, most of them more or less naked; with shouts and splashing, manœuvring the fragile net, they near the shore; the long silvery mullet fling themselves into the air, trying to hurdle the obstacle, but some are stunned and tossed up at once onto the beach, the old, no longer buoyant crones racing along the sands to where they fall, catching them before they can flop back into the surf.

A look of delight comes into the eyes of the present country people when asked whether they go to the coast in the summer. And one pictures the fires around the mouths of the bays, the chance to meet friends, the sun and change of diet, and the excitement of searching for shellfish amongst the waves, and how freshened they must feel as, with their camels and children, and a last can of mussels, they once again reach their hot dusty farms. Something of the old Mahoh probably rises to the surface as they range the familiar coast. Long before Europeans were first allowed time off to take seaside holidays, the custom was current in Fuerteventura.

There is now interference with the islanders' outings. Land-speculators and other foreigners have found that the *chozas* are, as one would expect, in desirable bays. But, by ancient custom, the builder of one of these shanties is the owner of it, though not of the ground, and cannot be evicted, at least by the ordinary landowner. The test case is in the ownership of the houses of the fishing village of Pozo Negro—one of the places marked on the

Venetian Giacomo Giroldi's 1426 map. At Pozo Negro, the long-unquestioned users of the houses claim them : so does the relevant *ayuntamiento*, whose coastal area it is. The *ayuntamiento* wants to sell off Pozo Negro to the tourism exploiters. So, for that matter, do the house 'owners'. Only money is at stake in the matter of the Pozo Negro dwellings; there is an injunction against touching any of them, a decision being awaited from Madrid. But the humble *chozas'* fate is clearly tied to that of these rather better houses. Nevertheless, even if legally cleared off, one senses that the mussel-hunters will still return each summer, and that the incoming owner of a new chalet can expect to find them still wading about on the surf-line and 'making the place hideous' with their songs and bottles, shell-mounds and cheap worn-out shoes.

TRUFFLE HUNTING

Figures with heads bent, ambling up, down, along a hillside, are usually hunting for truffles, *criadas*. A little rain and the fungus is at once to be found, becoming plentiful after ten days. The sun-rose acts as the pig of the island truffler : 'If you want to find truffles, look for the *turmeras*. . . .' The native, yellow-flowered *Helianthemum canariense* is a little blue-green plant, the most inconspicuous imaginable. But whole stretches of the *barranco* slopes are covered in it, so there is plenty of ground to hunt over. Here and there amongst the *turmeras* the earth gets pushed up a little, as by a nascent mushroom, though nothing is visible. The hunter scrapes away and reveals a cracked greyish-brown lump, the size of a medium potato, though they can be as large as a fist. The truffle is nearest a large puff-ball in aspect. There is no apparent connection with the *turmeras*, which are often not at all close, and in fact truffles can be found in the Jandía Jable dunes, where the *turmera* does not live; but this is considered simply freakish.

'They're funny, just made of water and earth, no seed or anything!' A rhyme about them puns on the names used in the two extreme islands.

FUERTEVENTURA

> *'Soy "nacida" en La Palma*
> *Y "criada" en Fuerteventura*
> *Sin cruzar el mar*
> *Sin hueso y sin coyuntura.'*

'I'm "born" in La Palma and "reared" in Fuerteventura, without crossing the sea, with neither bone nor joint.' Cooked like potatoes, they are as good if not better, with their light flavour of smoked bacon. Many local people collect the truffles; they are sold for 5 pesetas a kilo, to be passed on eventually to the Las Palmas public at 50. The shepherds enjoy competing for them, for 'the day goes very slowly up here, just watching the animals'.

PROPER NAMES

On the southern coast of the Jandía Jable, the land-merchants have erected a noticeboard: Costa Calma, to be the dunes' market name. The Calm Coast, reassuring. At the turnings down to the first chalets there are glossy little letterboxes on poles, each one with a new gilt lock, the foreigners' names neatly painted. A dozen 'Villa Mañanas' are indicated, across the desert.

Taken overall, the proper names of a people often of course reflect their history and their current outlook and aspirations. On Fuerteventura one notes in the proper names too the contrast between the European and the traditional. The one group is a mirror of intricate commercial and cultural subtleties, the other a reflection of simplicity. The names of places and animals can be taken as illustrations.

The idea of actually *thinking up* a name for something is quite foreign to the islanders; this was once so everywhere, of course. Places on Fuerteventura are obviously what they are: Mountains of Pass If You Can, The Headland One Avoids—Punta La Que Se Huye—and Juan Gomez's Beach. Montaña Sin Nombre, Without-a-Name Mountain, seems to underline this complete lack of a desire to invent names. But now things are changing, the renaming of the capital is a sure sign of this. Over five hundred years old, older than Las Palmas and Santa Cruz de Tenerife, an

180

earlier colony than New York or Sydney, Puerto Cabras, Goat Port, was thought too ugly a name to stay—although no shepherd will be found who agrees—and it has just become Port of the Rosary. Though the place itself, alas, is steadily becoming more hideous, not less so, a rosary strung with shacks of naked concrete. The island authorities wanted to rename their capital after a past king, which may have had unacceptable political implications. But it was the regional bishop who decided it, though he didn't even live on Fuerteventura. Yet the goats have had far more positive influence on Fuerteventura than the church. Responsible for the utter lack of vegetation, the 'poor men's cows' have paid for it with milk and cheese, fats and meat, and provided containers and clothing, and even fed the children of not a few. But bourgeois shame and the erection of the blinker-façade for tourists has made all reference to the goaty past—and present—offensive. To the despair of many a map-maker, Puerto Cabras has been replaced by Puerto del Rosario.

Calling things by fanciful names is now spreading to other aspects of island life, though slowly. In the case of houses, for example, past custom has of course been that the first in each place bears its name, or perhaps names the place, as for example 'Barranco de los Canarios—the ravine of the Gran Canaria people. Any houses which come after are always just 'So-and-So's' or 'The Lower One' or 'The House with the Mill'. Not a sign of a 'Chez nous'. Equally, to put up the name on the house front, when it is simply a description of the obvious, would have been thought ridiculous, a waste of time and money; however, apart from the foreigners, the nascent bourgeoisie is starting to do so, the infrequent occasions being sometimes a metre or two long, in barely legible wrought-iron lettering.

The country people, who had no voice in the capital's change of name, still call a goat a goat. It is not necessary to give examples of the coy, fanciful or subtly-humorous names often given to European domesticated animals. On Fuerteventura, herd animals are not named, even the odd long-haired goat provoking no more than 'El Peludo'—The Hairy One. Donkeys

181

come next : they do need distinguishing and so usually are either 'Moreno', 'Negro' or 'Pardo' . . . Brown, Black or Drab. Cats are about at the same level. Dogs, however, usually receive special names, but certainly not always. Such as are heard are dignified : Paisano or Comrade, Buen Amigo or Good Friend, Capitán or Captain. To suggest they might be called by human names, like Tomás or Xavier, is to bring cries of indignation : 'What ! Those names are only for Christians !'

PRIVACY

The pre-conquest Canary Islanders, said Glas, 'had a custom among them, that when one person went to the house of another, he did not attempt to enter it, but either whistled or sang till someone came out and desired him to walk in.' When paying a courtesy call on another farmhouse, the present country people halt far from the door, often a terrace below, and simply clap their hands or shout *'Buenos días!'* until someone appears. They do not knock on the door, or even go up to it.

ATTITUDES

Two attitudes of the *majoreros*, as the islanders call themselves, need clearer definition, those towards their pre-conquest ancestors and their present centralised dictatorship.

A chance remark of a farmer leads to speculation on the first : 'It was wrong to take away their land.' And, on the second, the words of an old shepherd, in a lowered voice : 'I heard on the radio that there was a chance that the Spanish would exchange some unimportant island for Gibraltar. . . .' He laughs, but seems nevertheless quite serious when he goes on : 'Perhaps they'd swop it for Fuerteventura—then something would get done here, there'd be work all right. This government does almost nothing for us.' In case this conversation seems unlikely, here is a quotation from Olivia Stone's visit to the islands almost a century ago : 'Don Manuel and many more of his countrymen would

182

give much to see the Canary Islands in the possession of England'. She also added that many people thought it a pity that Nelson did not capture Tenerife, for all that the flags he lost in the battle had become objects of worship. In 1902 troops had to be called in to suppress an autonomy movement in the Canaries. There is at present a 'Mouvement pour l'Autodétermination et l'Indépendence de l'Archipel Canarién', based in Algiers. Isolation incubates independence.

12 POST-CONQUEST EUROPEAN INTEREST

ONCE firmly colonised by the Spanish, and not worth international conflict, Fuerteventura was soon forgotten by the other European nations. Even peninsular Spain had little idea of the true nature and life of the island, to judge by the translator of the 'Tristan' legend. Throughout several centuries and right up to the recent land-rush, only the English vied with the Moors in their interest in Fuerteventura.

ENGLISH PIRATES, 1740

Two major English expeditions once landed at the nearby port of Gran Tarajal within a month of each other : 80 of the men were killed and the other 20 taken prisoner. For they came with no other aim than to pillage, the limit of the English interest, in 1740, in 'The Sun-kissed Isles of the Atlantic'.

With drums beating, trumpets sounding, colours flying, the two extraordinarily similar expeditions marched up the broad *barranco* bed. At Casilla Blanca the English proto-tourists paused and, very correctly, asked for a guide, allowing a local priest to send ahead 'a slave' with a warning. The pirates soon reached and set about looting Tuineje, the first large village in their way. One wonders whether they found any more there than the Earl of Cumberland's men who, in 1596, had attacked the capital of Lanzarote and, says Glas, found nothing but 'a small quantity of cheese and wine and whole reams of popish bulls and pardons'. Whilst the 1740 pirates were busy in Tuineje, the Fuerteventura

184

militia was roused, the able-bodied population marshalled, the retreat cut off. The English pirates, in the second foray under the ship's lieutenant, who is quaintly recorded by the Spanish as 'M. Ja. Mor. Benabar Bill', formed up and, with drums beating and trumpets sounding again, began to march back to the harbour, exhibiting all the signs of calm over-confidence. On the first occasion, the island horde, armed in the old Mahoh style with sticks and stones, forced them to halt and fight. The English, no doubt grouped geometrically and without a touch of panic, raised their muskets and fired at the charging rabble. Alas, the thoughtful islanders were unsportingly attacking behind a line of camels and these took the musket balls. Before the English could reload, the staves and stones were amongst them : thirty dead, the other twenty prisoners. On the second occasion the furious islanders, with the victory of only a month earlier still fresh, simply fell upon the English as they were leaving Tuineje, and massacred all fifty on the spot. Island dead were few on each occasion. To record the triumphs, a number of long and oddly identical statements, couched in flowing literary terms, were made by local combatants, each one however ending 'not signed by me because I can't write'. Pensions were awarded by the King to all involved; the recipients spent several years attempting to draw them.

It is a curious fact that the time of the Gibraltar trouble should coincide with the publication of a book of 164 pages, probably the largest publication ever devoted entirely to the island, entitled 'English Attacks upon Fuerteventura, 1740'. Following the somewhat misleading title, it begins : 'One cannot serve Spain better than by studying the episodes of which her History is full. . . .'

LAND

Land is now the dominant single topic in the island. Vast coastal zones—not just shoreline strips—are being acquired by the speculators in tourism. The effect on the islanders is twofold, material and mental. To understand the present position it is necessary to consider the history of island land-tenure, illustrated by the case which has aroused greatest indignation and resistance, that of the Jandía. In an atmosphere of suspicion over the many land deals, hostile to the enforced changes in their way of life, the people watch the influx of foreigners and wait for the future to come to them.

Already by 1506 a law had been passed at the Spanish Court which shows that a tendency had begun which, in spite of the legislation, has continued up to the present day. The law said that, because land and water in the Canaries were not justly shared out, the 'powerful' having taken over huge areas of the best land without just title, in future there could be no legal transfer of property by the poor to the rich or to people foreign to the islands : *'Que no se venda ingenio ni heredamiento a persona poderoso ni de fuera de estas islas.'* But the law was not only too late for the Mahohs who survived the conquest : if, by 1506, the Lord of Fuerteventura, Bethencourt's current successor, held the best part of the island and extracted the *quinto*, or fifth of the value, on all exports, by 1887 the island had come to be owned 'almost entirely' by one man, according to Olivia Stone. By 1506 the poor, a mixture of Mahoh and Moorish slaves and serfs together with the unsuccessful amongst the European immigrants, were already the poor. Twentieth-century land tenure is clearly in line with this history. On the one hand the vast majority, the shepherds and farmers, most with just enough land to survive off . . . *if* it rains. On the other hand, a few land-owners whose property is large enough to repay the capital investment needed to raise water from the depths at all times of the year . . . and who engage on minimum terms the rain-awaiting country people. The poor can never acquire property from the rich, but the latter are constantly absorbing land left by those agriculturalists who give up the struggle and go. And here of course, as in the Hebrides and many of the world's depressed areas, is another cause of the pessimism of the shepherds and farmers. This is the background.

The position when the first speculators arrived was that the title to all or almost all of the coastal zone was divided between a few rich private owners and the island *ayuntamientos*, the regional councils; the whole of this land was grazed by the people's flocks, that of the private owners for varied returns, that of the local authorities being common and available to the respective parishioners. The individual owners began selling out at once; the *ayuntamientos*, whose holdings in this game of desert monopoly were somewhat the less sandy and legally rather the more complicated, have entered the market more recently. Amongst the vast areas acquired by the speculators are the already-noted Costa Calma of the Jandía, the coast north of Cotillo and, in the north-east, the sand wastes of the Jable del Moro; presumably because 'The Moor's Dunes' might raise disagreeable images for lady bathers, the investors have hastily daubed 'Solyplayas' on the map, Sun-and-Beaches. Building has begun, the foreigners arrive in a steady stream, unaware of the clash between the interests, on the one hand, of their *conquistadores* and themselves and, on the other, of the islanders.

As an illustration which centres on the most general point of contention—grazing rights—the peculiar evolution of the Jandía land-title can be described. Within living memory the peninsula has been a place to which, in time of drought, the country people could take or send their flocks. However, unlike the undesirable lava-fields, an alternative resort, the Jandía is often very good pasture indeed. Doubtless the fifteenth century's first European overlords, from Bethencourt to Herrera, got the 'legal' title of most of it for themselves. Anyway, certain it is that the Jandía has long passed out of the control of the common people. Nevertheless, although, unlike much of the lava-fields, not 'common-land', the Jandía has always been grazed. There are many long-established settlements there, including the village of Morro Jable of course, and there has always been a public road right to the end.

About the time of the Civil War, ownership of the whole immense peninsula, some 200sq km, was transferred to a German. Suggestively beside the kingdom-dividing wall of the Mahohs, and as unique in the island, a head-high barrier of sixteen lines of double-ply heavily-barbed wire was then erected across the

5km-wide isthmus, from shore to shore. A gate under the control
of an employee was placed across the public road to the settlements. The grazing was on the half-profits system, which in this
case is to say that in order to pasture his own animals each
islander had to care for as many of the owner's and take him
their yield : it seems that few, if any, north-end flock owners have
since gone down to graze their animals in the Jandía.

The next stage came with the arrival of the speculators a few
years ago. Tomato cultivation in the Jandía being tried about
then and failing, government permission was obtained to turn
the peninsula into a tourism-development zone. The owner
started to sell off great tracts of the Jandía to the foreign investors. In order to present the rugged landscape in a guise which
would appeal to potential buyers of holiday-chalets, the speculators planted a few trees along the shore. The Jandía people's
sheep and goats, free-roaming over the *jable*, ate them; the trees,
anyway very few, could have been protected at a small cost compared to the money being made out of the land deals. The speculators had been sold not merely the shore but the hinterland
too, and they had the several thousand animals rounded up and
cleared off. The drought was at its maximum, after three years
without adequate rain, and there was no other grazing. The
people had to sell their animals as best they could. The middlemen whose seasonal business is to buy up starving drought-
struck animals no doubt offered 'highest prices'. Numerous families lost an important part of their food and livelihood, and
capital. The author read the official clearance notices at Morro
Jable and witnessed the village's open hositility towards foreigners,
and saw a great flock of the animals being taken away by a
middleman for shipment.

The 1506 law, wise and just, strikingly on the side of the poor,
was enacted to avoid such an event : by a series of mutations the
use of the land has passed out of the hands of the people. Grazing on the northern Jable del Moro was also immediately for-
bidden by the speculators. The Jandía islanders have begun a
lawsuit, which they will probably lose : to carry it against big

business interests needs much money, and anyway tourism development is part of the State's policy.

But it is not only that each chalet advertisement in a northern country represents the death warrant of a flock of goats. Coupled to the islanders' loss of livelihood there is—due to the impact of the foreigners—both a rise in the general cost of living, with the local fishermen unable to afford to build houses on their own shores, because of the soaring land-prices of course, and an increase in the desired standard of material life. This drives the country people, in particular those affected by 'the clearances', to leave the land and work as quarrymen and builders, as servants and barmen, which of course exactly suits the requirements of the new order. And thus yet another culture is shattered by commercial interests. A Jandía shepherdess summed up the attitude of the indignant, bewildered islanders : 'We don't mind the foreigners coming, there's plenty of room for all of us, but they shouldn't interfere with our way of life.'

Petty suspicion over land deals is widespread. For instance, a foreign speculator, who has long left the island, agreed with a group of mountain people to buy their land and pay them for it once he had sold it on to his distant countrymen. Although the land was a few hundred metres up and several kilometres of deep, arid, trackless ravines from the Atlantic, the sea *was* just distinguishable in the distance, and it appears that the speculator's prospectus misled the intending, distant purchasers . . . however, luckily for them, they seem to have got together to send an agent out to look the land over. Still in possession of their mountainous territory, these islanders too greet foreigners and suggested land deals with reserve.

Mushrooming multi-coloured chalets are to be seen dotting the dunes and low cliffs of Fuerteventura's once deserted coastline. Most of the owners seem to be Germans, some are English and other nationalities; a very few are Spanish. The material effect on the islanders has been gauged and illustrated, but the mental result of the constant presence of the materially more-evolved foreigners is less easy to measure and depict.

Imagine the effect on, say, the islanders of Skye, to suddenly find that somehow or other the best part of their coastline has been sold to Italian developers, who are making enormous profits selling it on to other Italians, French, Germans and Spaniards in smaller plots. Few Scots can afford to buy any of the land—to continue the analogy—and the proud, dour crofters have the choice of becoming builders and servants or making nothing out of it at all. Huge glossy southern European cars, crammed with well-fed, well-dressed unintelligible people, now appear on the island. As the houses go up—palaces at the side of the ancient island dwellings, let us say—and the crofters take in for the first time the model bathrooms, the electricity motors and water-pumps, the immense windows and the luxurious terraces, and the money-careless fantasies of each owner, they are forced to realise their own 'backwardness'. These houses, they say to themselves, are these people's *holiday* homes. Portree, Skye's capital, is soon riddled with mock-Spanish *bodegas*, pseudo-French *bistros*, and, perhaps the worst, 'genuine Skye whisky bars'. A Levantine from Tangier is to open a night club on an artificial island in the middle of the harbour. The trouble, grumble the men of Skye, is the exchange rate, to hand out £168 for each of those pesetas gives the Spaniards an unfair advantage. Somehow the common grazing which the crofters have enjoyed since the days of Bonnie Prince Charlie has got into the hands of a group of Italians and these have just had all the Highland cattle caught and cleared off . . . but 'they'—in London—do nothing about it, as usual, 'they' don't care, are probably all for it in fact. There's a new hotel going up in pink granite and it's to be exactly the same shape as Dunvegan Castle, an Arab airline's doing it, and training batches of crofters' daughters as waitresses, in Casablanca.

In addition to the wages the islanders earn working for tourism, the island as a community benefits from the sale of *ayuntamiento* land, though not of course from that of the large estates. The *ayuntamiento* money will swell the funds available for improvements in the island, where, as the Island Council or Cabildo 1960

190

'Memoria' states, the people's standard of living is *en un sesenta o setenta por ciento, rayano en la miseria*—for sixty or seventy per cent, on the brink of penury. But will the land-sale income be high enough to achieve anything lasting for Fuerteventura? On the neighbouring island of Lanzarote, the administration found that it was holding the Park Lane and Mayfair of the game, the golden dunes just across the Bocayna Strait from Fuerteventura: the selling prices of which the author heard, risible compared to the selling-on prices of the developers, were *a peseta a square metre*, less than one new penny. One hopes the Fuerteventura *ayuntamientos* will do better than this: already in December 1966 a tourist-exploitation company was asking 15,000 pesetas a month for a chalet near Corralejo and, since the Canaries' season lasts the whole year round, this is about £1,000 per annum. The new *conquistadores* are not after the goats. That the islanders are providing the labour force in the tourism development is no more a justification than in the case of the conquest of the prehistoric islanders: they are working for their wages and, until return for labour in Spain catches up with that in the rest of Europe, working per peseta rather harder than those who are paying them. In the absence of Sancho Panza's powers, the Cabildo and the *ayuntamientos*, and of course the government, should try every available means to adequately recompense the islanders for what is presumably the permanent loss of their land. Tourist-exploiter or tourist, most do not comprehend the islanders' lives; at the best a few experience a passing benevolence marginal to the pleasures for which they have come. And it will all go on for just as long as the sun shines regularly upon the thirtieth parallel.

MODERN TOURISM

Facilities are wider than in the time of Captain Glas, who preferred to keep his ship as a base, or during the visit of Olivia Stone, who did not enjoy her crossing in a small boat and carried out her tour on horseback. The present service of aeroplanes and

191

steamers and the number of hotels, pensions and chalet each increase steadily as more and more people visit Fuerteventura. Internal transport ranges from scheduled bus services through taxis to the hire of bicycles and camels. For seasonal information the visitor should contact either the Casa del Tourismo, Las Palmas, Grand Canary or the Spanish Tourist Office, Jermyn Street, London.

As an example of a seaside resort, in fact Fuerteventura's most vaunted, Corralejo, opposite Isla Lobos, can be described. The setting—craters, the Atlantic, the little island across the strait, Lanzarote to the north—is unsurpassed in the Canaries. The village, however, is unattractive and quite without interest. Why anyone should wish to spend any time there until its development is over and the dust and noise have died down is not clear; since building is piecemeal in such a long-established village, a visitor or a purchaser can wake up any day to find a house or a hotel starting a metre or two away. Corralejo will long be simply a spreading building site, dominated by concrete mixers, lorries, floating discarded cement bags, falling rubble and staring whistling oafs.

On Corralejo's jetty old fishermen sit angling for wrasse. Minute launches dot the horizon, some off Isla Lobos. A boat can always be found to cross to the little island, at a cost of some 500 pesetas when the minimum daily wage stood at 84. Things have changed since Gadifer, trading with the Canary Islanders, received quantities of figs and dragon tree sap worth 200 ducats and in exchange gave fish hooks, needles and old iron tools 'all of it not worth two francs'. He'd have to bring something better nowadays.

In fact Fuerteventura has really only one of the typical resort attractions : its sunny, sandy beaches, of which the finest have been described. The way visitors spend their time lying on the beaches astonishes the islanders, underlines the vast gulf between them and the strangers. One hears '. . . and have you seen them on the beaches? Without any clothes on, I mean, or hardly any!' Again '. . . and it's surprising they let it go on'.

192

POST-CONQUEST EUROPEAN INTEREST

But the islanders know Spain is seeking tourists, and tourists would not come if they couldn't sunbathe on the beaches. '*El dinero allana todo*', they say. Money smoothes everything. The island's interest, in fact, does not lie in night clubs and other resort entertainments, nor in quaint 'old quarters' nor in immediately-appealing landscapes; neither do its people ply traditional crafts or wear typical costume. The island is more subtly engrossing, holding out not the striking, lightning attraction of a young woman but the lasting flavour of the stories of an old crone at her fireside.

A BALANCED FUTURE

THE island's main characteristics can now be summarised. The geology, almost entirely volcanic; the geography, a matter of bare windswept mountains, lava-fields and dunes which surround a fertile but usually dry plain. The archaeology : probably the first important immigration came from North Africa shortly after the time of Christ. The recorded 1402–5 conquest of the Mahohs and the appropriation of the island by Europeans. The disappearance of the pre-conquest people, during the fifteenth century. Their replacement as slaves by more people from Africa, the result of man-hunts on the adjacent coast during the late fifteenth and sixteenth centuries. The period since : many of them slaves and serfs until not long ago, the islanders' lives have been moulded, in total isolation, by chronic drought and other lesser calamities, the results of which have been the interlocking of hunger, pessimism and dependence upon herding and farming in an island almost devoid of vegetation and water. This leaves the present.

The island's isolation is now at an end. Progress, in its material and non-material aspects, is now a possibility. Materially, there are already signs of change. The government, whatever the island people may say, is no longer inactive there, especially when one bears in mind the small size of the population and the limitations of Spain's resources. Franco 'adopted' the island in the early 1950s, promising some 70 million pesetas over three years; by 1960 the improvements were still in infancy, according to an official publication, and the author does not know whether any summary of results has been issued, so that what follows is purely a personal impression. There are many new schools, there are schemes like the tree plantations in the mountains and the fibre cultivation on the plain. Plenty of roads have been made. Work to improve irrigation, by constructing reservoirs and making deep soundings, is destined to fail only because the government can neither cause rain to fall nor the water-table to rise to a height capable of economic exploitation. The Navy brings in drinking water. A state pension scheme exists. The state's new tourism constructions, an airfield and a Parador, have indirectly provided work, and so have loans for the making of hotels. Government agricultural advice and assistance is available; this includes the hire of tractors at low rates and courses to teach the farmers to get the best from their land. Apart from the state schemes, individual enterprise is bringing work. For example, capital invested in private chalets and general tourist-exploitation. Tomato cultivation, fairly new in this island and steadily increasing, employs many, both in the plantations and as packers. Local unions and marketing co-operatives should see to it that their members receive a fair and steady offer for their work and produce.

However, from a European point of view—by which the island would wish to be judged—Fuerteventura is still very backward materially. The average income is far below even that of the rest of the nation. Diet is poor. Water chronically short. Bus services are insufficient, private cars are few, many roads are very rough. Only the larger villages have electricity and then can afford only a meagre lighting for the first few hours each night; the poorer people's houses do not have adequate provision for natural lighting. There is no evening education of the adult country people. Facilities for the poor to obtain technical or professional training are negligible. Agriculture, pastoralism and fishing are usually primitive and poorly rewarding. The hospital has only four beds and no permanent staff, and many have to go to Gran Canaria for treatment. Public sports and recreation facilities do not exist. The island exchequer, official publications show, just does not have the money to do any more.

Before coming to the most obvious source on which the needy island should draw, the non-material aspect of the people's lives can be considered. What, in this way, have the 1960s brought the islanders? Not very much. Luckily, the desire to have their children educated, perhaps the most valuable of investments; though the schools are still very limited. Otherwise, a walk through the two towns simply reveals a great influx of the junk of civilisation. Free time and the creative spirit are offered photos of film stars, adult-aimed comics, ball pens, ornamental plastic garlics, discs of popular music, violence-accustoming toys. But there is no bookshop and the library has only about 3,000 books, the majority out-of-date fiction. Advertising increases steadily. Most families have radios, but there is no island newspaper, and thus no regular community expression. There are television clubs, but no live association for playing music or acting; there is a cinema or two, but no group which actively takes an interest in the countryside or in the island's past. Traditional entertainments are reduced to singing or dancing for television or radio. Modern dances, with the very occasional football and wrestling match, and a church pilgrimage now and then, are the only organised public gatherings. Encouragement of crafts is limited to purely commercial embroidery and dressmaking, of arts there is none; the professional craftsmen, lacking a co-operative, are all but entirely superseded by outside factories, but there is no sign that making things as ends in themselves, like pots and pictures, is known. Tourist-exploitation grows steadily, but, apart from two teach-yourself sets of language discs at the capital's library, there is no stimulus or desire to travel, or to understand the foreigners and their homelands. The small new museum is simply a store-house, though a pleasant one, for island relics—few country people have been there, and anyway they are still using most of the objects exhibited. In fact, there is no sign whatsoever of adult cultural advance.

That there is a lack of public money is, of course, true. The state has plenty of other areas in need of help, the island cannot expect £40,000 very often, assuming the Adoption scheme actually spent the sum it promised. The total 1960 budget of the island Cabildo amounted to only £11,000, a little over sixty

196

pence a head. A Sancho Panza, in charge of this desert and poverty-stricken Barataria, would not hesitate for long over the solution. Half the profit on each successful speculation by the tourist-exploiters would have to be devoted to public works around the island. Sancho would underline the unfairness of the spectacle of outsiders, now as ever indifferent to the lot of the island people, making vast profits—that on a single chalet sale is probably greater than a month of the combined budgets of the island *ayuntamientos* and Cabildo—whilst the islanders simply lose the use of the land. To the mass of the Fuerteventura poor, conditioned by centuries of hunger and failure into pessimistic resignation, it is not surprising that their island, until recently dismissed as dross, should, thanks to the modern sun worshippers, be suddenly turned into gold by strangers : on Fuerteventura things are like that, nobody expects anything else.

The present transactions and manœuvres have only two parallels in importance in the island's past, the landing of the first of the pre-historic people and then, at least a thousand years later, the moment when Gadifer de la Salle came ashore. The day the first land-speculator arrived may be seen by future historians as the beginning of a second conquest, followed by nothing better than the only form of colonialism now open to northerners, purchase of advantageously priced land in an underdeveloped country. It is certain that, in spite of himself, the land-speculator's appearance will help the islanders towards independence : not towards that of an indigenous people from their distant rulers, since the Mahohs, like the rest of the pre-conquest Canary islanders, were erased almost as thoroughly as were the Tasmanians by the British, but towards independence from the goats and the rain. However, will Fuerteventura profit sufficiently to be able to bring about that modernisation of work and education-level which will ensure that the islanders avoid becoming in turn as dependent on the northerners as they were on the goats and the rain before ? It is arguable which is the better of the two fates, but it is certain that a more balanced state than either is preferable. Whatever the outcome, it seems likely that for Fuerteventura the present years are a period in which a first phase of human activity overlaps with a second.

The safest plan for the material future of the island would probably be made up of three roughly *equal* parts. More advanced agriculture, pastoralism and fishing; light industries, to be established; tourism, bearing in mind that the island belongs, ethically at least, to the islanders.

Development of the non-material side seems to be all but forgotten, as in many a materially-evolving place—and, since the tourist trade will appear to many to be the fastest way to prosperity, there is more than a chance that a touting materialism will come to dominate the thoughts of the people, though particularly in the ports and other tourism zones, as everywhere in the world. In Fuerteventura one would like to see prosperity and advance, without materialism. The country dwellers at least have as much chance as any of achieving this, for—and to assess this judgement one must live amongst them—they are an austere yet generous people, shrewd but trusting, humble yet straight-standing, ignorant only because they have not been taught and otherwise strong in intelligence and understanding, in openness and immediate friendliness.

APPENDIX I

PLANTS ON A SHEPHERD'S PASTURE

THE following are the most important plants, excluding the few grasses, noted between the western outskirts of Antigua and the top of the western cordillera. To these should be added all plants mentioned in Chapter 2 except the five *jable* species, *Euphorbia canariensis*, *E. handiensis* and *Limonium ?papillatum* (hybrid).

Adonis microcarpa, Aeonium percarneum, Aizoön canariense, Anagallis arvensis var. *caerulea, Anchusa italica, Andryala ?cheiranthifolia, Arabis* sp.*, Calendula aegyptiaca, Centaurea lippa, C. melitensis, Chenopodium murale, Chrysanthemum coronarium, Cichorium divaricatum, Convolvulus althaeoides, Coriandrum sativum, Cuscuta* sp.*, Echium ?plantagineum, Erodium malacoides, Fagonia cretica, Forskohlea angustifolia, Frankenia capitata, Gladiolus* sp.*, Glaucium corniculatum, Gomphocarpus fruticosus, Heliotropium erosum* var. *prostratum, Hirschfeldia incana, Inula viscosa, Launaea nudicaulis, Limonium thouinii, Linaria ?scoparia, Lotus* sp.*, Lythrum hyssopifolium, Malva nicaeënsis (?), Matthiola parviflora, Mentha* sp.*, Ononis pendula* var. *canariensis, Orobanche ?ramosa, Pallenis spinosa, Papaver rhoeas, Picridium* sp. (?)*, Psoralea bituminosa, Raphanes raphanistrum, Reseda scoparia, Ricinus communis, Rumex lunaria, R. vesicarius, Salsola vermiculata, Salvia aegyptiaca, S. clandestina, Scorpiurus sulcatus, Solanum nigrum, Urticaceae* sp..

APPENDIX II

THE BIRDS

The following list is based upon *Birds of the Atlantic Islands* Vol. 1, by David A. Bannerman. The present writer has added the Cabrera's blackbird, its first recording on Fuerteventura.

Breeding: Blackbird, Cabrera's; Bullfinch, Canarian trumpeter; Bunting, Thanner's corn; Bustard, Fuerteventura houbara; Buzzard, Canarian; Chat, Meade-Waldo's; Courser, Canarian; Dove, common turtle; Falcon, Barbary; Falcon, Eleanora's; Goldfinch, least or Madeiran; Gull, Atlantic; Hawk, Ogilvie-Grant's sparrow-; Hoopoe; Kestrel, Fuerteventuran; Lark, Polatzek's short-toed; Linnet, Hartert's; Osprey; Owl, slender-billed barn; Oystercatcher, Meade-Waldo's black; Partridge, Koenig's Barbary; Pigeon, Canarian rock; Pipit, Berthelot's; Plover, Kentish; Quail, migratory; Raven, Tangier; Sandgrouse, western black-bellied; Shearwater, Cory's or Atlantic; Shrike, Koenig's great grey; Sparrow, Spanish; Swift, Brehm's; Swift, Madeiran black; Tern, common; Thick-knee, eastern Canarian; Titmouse, pale or Fuerteventuran; Vulture, Egyptian; Warbler, Canary spectacled; Warbler, Sardinian (Canarian race).

Others recorded: Bee-eater, common; Blackcap, European; Bluethroat; Chiffchaffs, European (*P. collybita c.*, *P.c. brehmi*); Coot; Curlew; Dunlins (*C. alpina* [*a*],*C.a.* [*schinzii*]); Falcon, peregrine; Flamingo; Flycatchers, pied and spotted; Gannet; Godwits, black- and bar-tailed; Grebe, little; Heron, common grey; Kite; Lapwing; Lark, sky; Mallard; Martins, crag and house; Moorhen; Oystercatcher; Pipit, meadow; Plovers, grey and ringed; Pratincole, collared; Razorbill; Redbreast; Redstart; Redstart, black; Roller; Ruff; Sandpipers, common, curlew, green and wood; Snipe, common; Spoonbill; Stonechat; Stork, white; Swallow; Teal; Tern, little; Thrush, song; Turnstone; Wagtails, blueheaded (*M. flava* [*f.*], *M.f.* [*iberiae*]); Warblers, aquatic and willow; Wheatears (*Oenanthe oe.oe.*, *Oe. oe. leucorrhoa*); Whimbrel; Whinchat; Whitethroat.

APPENDIX III

ANCIENT RUINS

The sites are grouped under their nearest villages, these being listed roughly from north to south. Those numbered were visited by the author, details of the others coming from a simple list of diggings twenty years ago by the Provincial Commissar for Archaeology; no other reports could be found. All houses and dwelling caves visited had middens. All the stone circles seen by the author are listed as corrals; at unvisited sites the Commissar's descriptions *gambuesa* and *tagoror* have been retained. *Gambuesa*, explained in the text, means a public corral; *tagoror*, not correctly used for Fuerteventura, is Tenerife Guanche for a public assembly place.

The Mahohs' private corrals and *gambuesas* and the Guanche *tagorors* were all stone circles, but the last-named—an equivalent probably did exist on Fuerteventure—would often have been a mere outlining of the arena rather than a good-sized wall for penning animals. However, the need for building stone, the continuance of the *gambuesa* custom and other factors have made it hard to decide the age of an enclosure or to tell one type from another; also, some were probably *efeguenes*, places of worship. But most were certainly simple animal corrals.

Unfortunately, a number of the actual site names do not appear on the military map, and the visitor will have to ask his way once in the immediate region, bearing in mind that only people living very near the caves or ruins will have heard of them. The many relics passed to the Betancuria Museum bore their site's number.

D : dwelling caves   H : houses   C : corrals   G : *gambuesas*
T : *tagorors*   N : necropolis.   Preceded by '1' : one only.
La Oliva. Punta Aguda (28) : H.   Calderón Hondo (29) : H, C.
Cohón : caves (near Los Lajares).   Coto del Coronel : H, G, T,
tumuli, votive monuments (lava-field near Los Lajares).   Tisajoyre
and Villaverde : caves, G, T, tumuli (north of La Oliva).   Rosa de
los Negrines (31) : H, C.   Corral del Consejo (32) : D, 1H.   La
Matilla, Tindaya, Los Sesquenes, La Laguna : various (south of
La Oliva).
Tetir. La Culata : H.   Tablero Blanco : H, G, 1T, temple.
Puerto del Rosario. Barranquillo de Lajas Azules : H, G, T,
burials, votive obelisks.   Majada del Viso : H, G, T.   Cerro del
Cuchillete and Llano del Biscocho : H (including square ones), G,
T, burials.   Lesque de la Pila : H, 1T, votive stone table.   Taima :
H, T.   La Herradura and Casas Altas : H, 1T, tumulus, votive
stone, possible inscriptions.   Barranco de Río Cabras : H, T, N.
La Guirra : H, G, T, N.
Casillas del Angel. Pico de la Fortaleza : D, H, T.   Lomo
Gordo : H, G, T.   Bajamanga (or Bocamanga), La Laguna and
Zurita : D, H, T.
Betancuria. Hoya del Dinero, Llanos de Sta. Catalina and La
Atalaya : burial cave, ruins.   Grano de Oro (33) : burial cave.
Castillo de Lara (26) : midden.
Antigua. Montaña del Sombrero (34) : foundations.   Lesque (25):
midden (see Appendix 4).   Pozo Santo : H (Antigua village—
destroyed?).   El Cortijo (15) : ruin.   Cueva de Punta Goma (5) :
1D, H.   Cueva del Roque del Besey (or Buey) : cave, H (near
Valles de Ortega).
Barranco de la Torre. El Esquen, Barranco de la Muley (3) :
H, C.   Miraflor : H, G, T, votive stone table.   Las Salinas : fish-
trap (El Corral).   Barranco de la Torre : (1) H, C (northern slope,
3km from coast); (11) H, C, disinterred construction (Rosita del
Vicario); (24) 1H (Fuente de las Ovejas); H (mouth, southern
side).   Caleta de la Ballena (7) : midden.   Caleta del Horno (12) :
midden.
Pozo Negro and coast southwards. Punta Leandro (2) : H, C.
El Saladillo (8) : H, C.   Cueva de los Vallichuelos : cave.   Gran
Valle del Barranco de las Cuevas : H, with labyrinthine linking, G,
T, tumulus burials, family votive table, liturgical table (probably
'Valle de la Cueva' or 'Gran Valle', both on map).   Toneles : H, N.
Valle de Jacomar : H, G.
Tiscamanita. Caldera de Gairía : burial cave.   Parrado (10) :

collapsed D? Malpaís Chico (27): 1D. Malpaís Grande (4):
D. Caldera de la Laguna (6) : 1D.

Tuineje. Barranquillo del Pozo : H, burials. Cuevas de Tenicosquey, del Castillejo, de las Paredejas, de la Chillona : caves. Corral
de los Asnos and Iglesia de los Majos : 1 C, temple. Cueva de
Zamorín : cave. Tiquital (map's Teguitar?), Caldera Los Arrabales
and Mar Rubio : H, T.

Pájara. Risco del Carnicero (9) : 1D, H, C. Llanos del Sombrero : H, including Casa del Rey (or Bey), G, T, tumuli, obelisk,
ceremonial bench, sacrificial table (between B. de la Peña and B. de
Ajui). Cuevas de Montaña Ancones, del Risco del Acebuche :
caves. Morrete de Mirabal (36) : 1H, 1C. Barranco de Vigocho
(13) : 1D, H, C. Barranco de Amanay : (16) H (watercourse); (30)
1H, 1C; (23) cliff midden.

Gran Tarajal. Monte Cardón (19) : fortified summit, D, H.
Barranco del Lomo Cumplido (17) : cave, 1H, 1C, tumuli. Ugán
(18) : midden.

Jandía. La Pared (35) : isthmus wall. Playa del Viejo Rey
(20) : H, 1C. Jable west coast (21) : H, C (several places). Barranco de Pezenescal : (22) H (upper); H (lower). Barrancos de los
Canarios, Esquinzo, Vinámar, Cofete, Pedro Alonso : H, in each.
Barranco de Munguía (14) : H, C.

BIBLIOGRAPHY

Abbreviations key:
AEA : Anuario de Estudios Atlánticos. Madrid-Las Palmas
AVCPP : Actas del V Congreso Panafricano de Prehistoria. Museo
Arqueológico, Tenerife
FRC : Fontes Rerum Canariarum. Tenerife
GJ : Geographical Journal. London
MC : El Museo Canario. Gran Canaria
RH : Revista de Historia. Tenerife
ABERCROMBY, J. 'The prehistoric pottery of the Canary Islands and
its makers.' *Journal of the Royal Anthropological Institute*, xliv.
London, 1914
ALMAGRO BASCH, M. *Prehistoria del Norte de África y del Sáhara
Español*. Instituto de Estudios Africanos. Barcelona, 1946
BANNERMAN, D. A. *Birds of the Atlantic Islands*. Oliver & Boyd.
Edinburgh, 1963
BENÍTEZ PADILLA, S. 'Origen más probable de las hachas neolíticas
de jadeita que posee el Museo Canario.' *AVCPP* I. 1965
BÉTHENCOURT, A., and RODRÍGUEZ, A. *Ataques ingleses contra
Fuerteventura*. Cabildo Insular de Fuerteventura. Valladolid,
1965
BONTIER, P., and LE VERRIER, J. *Le Canarien*. La Salle's version
(British Museum, MS Egerton 2709), ed P. Margry as *La Con-
quête des Canaries*. Leroux. Paris, 1896. Bethencourt's version
(Rouen, Mont Ruffet MS), trans. R. H. Major as *The Canarian*.
The Hakluyt Society. London, 1872
CENDRERO UCEDA, A. Los Volcanes Recientes de Fuerteventura,
Estudios Geológicos 22 (Dec 1966), 201–26.
CHAMORRO CUERVAS-MONS, M. *Plan de riegos y industralización
de las islas de Lanzarote y Fuerteventura*. Tenerife, 1951
CLASSE, A. *La fonética del silbo Gomero*. *RH*. 1959
CUSCOY, L. Diego. 'Noticias sobre el gofio de "vidrio".' *RH*, 79. 1947
DASH, B. P., and BOSSHARD, E. Crustal Studies around the Canary
Islands, *XXIII International Geological Congress*, vol 1 (1968),
249–60

205

BIBLIOGRAPHY

ESPINOSA, A. DE. *Historia de Nuestra Señora de Candelaria.* Tenerife, 1654

FERNANDES, V. *Das ilhas do mar oceano.* Portugal, 1507

FISCHER, E. 'Sind die alten Kanarien ausgestorben?' *Z. Ethnol,* 62. 1930

FORDE-JOHNSON, J. L. *Neolithic cultures of North Africa.* Liverpool University Press. Liverpool, 1959

FUSTÉ, M. 'Algunas observaciones acerca de la antropología de las poblaciones prehistórica y actual de Gran Canaria.' *MC,* 65–72. 1958–9

FUSTÉ, M. *Estudio antropológico de los esqueletos inhumados en túmulos de la región de Gáldar (Gran Canaria).* MC. 1963

FUSTÉ, M. 'Nuevas aportaciones a la antropología de Canarias.' *AVCPP* II. 1966

GALINDO, J. Abreu. *Historia de la conquista de las siete Islas de Canarias.* 1632—included in work by G. Glas

GLAS, G. *The history of the discovery and conquest of the Canaries.* Dodsley, London, 1764

HAUSEN, H. *On the geology of Fuerteventura.* Societas Scientiarum Fennica, Helsinki, 1958

HAUSEN, H. *Contribución al conocimiento de las formaciones sedimentarias de Fuerteventura (Islas Canarias).* AEA, 4, 1958

HOOTON, E. A. *The ancient inhabitants of the Canary Islands.* Peabody Museum, Harvard University. Cambridge, Mass, 1925

JÍMENEZ SÁNCHEZ, S. 'La prehistoria de Gran Canaria.' *RH,* 70. 1945

McBURNEY, C. B. M. *The stone age of Northern Africa.* Penguin Books, Harmondsworth, 1960

MARTÍNEZ SANTA-OLALLA, J. *África.* Seminario de Historia Primitiva del Hombre. Madrid, 1947

MATZNETTER, J. *Der Trockenfeldbau auf den Kanarischen Inseln.* Reviewed *RH,* 115–6. 1956

MURDOCK, G. P. *Africa, its peoples and their culture history.* McGraw-Hill. New York, 1959

PÉREZ DE BARRADAS, J. *Estado actual de las investigaciones prehistóricas sobre Canarias.* Madrid, 1938

ROBIN, J. 'Moors and Canary Islanders on the coast of the Western Sahara.' *GJ,* cxxi, Part 2, June. 1955.

ROLDÁN, R. *Acuerdos del Cabildo de Fuerteventura 1729–98. FRC,* XIV. 1966

ROTHE, P., and SCHMINCKE, H-U. Contrasting Origins of the Eastern and Western Islands of the Canarian Archipelago, *Nature*, vol 218 (June 22, 1968), 1152–1154

SCHAEFFER, H.-H. *Plants of the Canary Islands*. F. Kutscher. Ratzeburg, 1963

SCHWIDETZKY, I. 'Observaciones antropológicas en Tenerife (Relación de un viaje).' *RH*. 1956

SCHWIDETZKY, I. *La población prehispánica de las Islas Canarias*. El Museo Arqueológico. Tenerife, 1963

SERRA RAFOLS, E. *Acuerdos del Cabildo de Tenerife 1497–1507. FRC*, IV. 1949

SERRA RAFOLS, E. 'Los últimos canarios.' *RH*, 125–8. 1959

SERRA RAFOLS, E. 'El redescubrimiento de las Islas Canarias en el siglo catorce.' *RH*, 135–6. 1961

SERRA RAFOLS, E. Review of 14th edition of 'Brown's guide to the Canaries'. *RH*. 1964

STONE, O. *Tenerife and its six satellites*. 2 vols, 1887

TORRIANI, L.—included in work by D. J. Wolfel.

VIERA Y CLAVIJO, J. *Noticias de la historia general de las Islas Canarias*. Gran Canaria, 1772–3

WATKINS, N. D., RICHARDSON, A., and MASON, R. G. Palaeomagnetism of the Macaronesian Insular Region : the Canary Islands, *Earth and Planetary Science Letters* 1 (1966), 225–31

WOLFEL, D. J. *Leonardi Torriani. Die Kanarischen inseln und ihre unbekannte Bilderhandschrift vom Jahre 1590*. Leipzig, 1940

ZEUNER, F. E. 'Some domesticated animals from the prehistoric site of Guayadeque, Gran Canaria.' *MC*, 65–72. 1958–9

ZEUNER, F. E. *Líneas costeras del pleistoceno en las Islas Canarias. AEA*, 4. 1958

ZEUNER, F. E. 'Summary of the cultural problems of the Canary Islands.' *AVCPP* II. 1966

ZEUNER, F. E. 'The first fossil mammal from the Canary Islands.' *AVCPP* II. 1966

ACKNOWLEDGEMENTS

The field-work was fully shared by Susan Mercer, who also painted some eighty detailed water-colours used in identifying the island plants and helped with the general research. To her, then, is due much of this book.

Ninian Buchan-Hepburn is warmly thanked for providing the cover photograph. For discussion and identifications, the author is most grateful to the following: Dr H. M. Hausen and Dr P. Rothe (unrecorded volcanic glasses used as tools by the ancient islanders); Dr C. B. M. McBurney (North African archaeology); Prof C. N. Tavares (lichens); Royal Botanic Gardens, Kew; British Museum (Natural History); El Museo Canario (radio-carbon dates). Most of the pre-conquest material mentioned in the text was left on the sites, but some 550 decorated sherds and six unusual tools were passed to the Betancuria Museum; the nineteenth-century scene opening Chapter 10 is based on material in this museum.

There are two groups of people too numerous to be thanked individually. The writer gratefully acknowledges a debt to the authors who appear in the bibliography. And, finally, it is a pleasure to thank many of the people of Fuerteventura for their help and co-operation.

March 1972   Isle of Jura, Argyll, Scotland

INDEX

Numerals in italic refer to illustration pages

INDEX

Household objects, nineteenth-century, 148
Hunting, 37, 133, 174

Ibiza, 25, 81; dog species, 159
Ibn Khaldun, 62, 65
Idols and images, 42 55, 63, 140, 142, 170, 172
Ifni, 86–7, 97, 164
Immigration, modern, 197; Moors and Negroes, 86–8, 91–2; prehistoric, 29, 40–52, 55–63, 133; Spanish early post-conquest, 82
Imraguen, African tribe, 52, 87, 93
Incomes, modern, 154–6, 160, 163, 190, 192, 195
Inquisition, 91, 172
Inscriptions, prehistoric, 55–6
Insects, 21, 38, 120–3
Irrigation, 10, *108*, 135–6, 140, 150, 195
Isla Lobos, 27, 64, 68, 192

Jable, sand waste, 20–1
Jable de Jandía, 20
Jable del Moro, 27, 187–8
Jable de Vigocho, 20
Jadeite axes, 41, 59
Jandía peninsula, 21, 25, *35*, *53*, 180, 186–9
Jandía wall, *36*, 55, 104–5
Jews, expulsion of, 172
Juba II, King of Mauretania, 29, 44–6, 55, 63
Junquillo, 177

Kleinia neriifolia, 30

Laguna volcano, 15, 99–101
Land-holdings, 82–3, 94, 98, 141, 152, 178–9, 185–91, 197
Landscape, 9–16, *17–18*, 19–25, 35–6, *52*, *72*, *89*, *106*, *134*
Land–speculation, 21, 155, 158, 178–9, 185–91
Language, Castilian, 94–6, 167–9; early post-conquest, 94–6; pre-conquest, 29, 42, 55–8, 60–2, 73, 103, 158
Lanzarote, 13–14, 21, 25, 48, 56, 64–5, 67, 69, 76–7, 80, 86, 88, 92, 110, 145, 184, 191
La Oliva, 16, 32, *89*, *107*, 110, 123–30
La Palma, 33, 48, 50, 78, 80
La Salle, Gadifer de, 66–70, *71*, 72–8, 103, 192, 197

212

Las Hermosas, 160
Las Palmas, 180
Lava-fields, *see* Badlands
Leather industry, 142–3
Library, 196
Lichens, 32, 117–19, 208
Lime-burning, *18*, 19
Literacy, 168
Lizards, 21, 24, 167
Locust plague, 140
Loom, 165
Los Lajares, 24, 151
Lugo, Alonso de, 78–9, 81

Madrague, 177–8
Mahohs, 10, 25, 65, 133; beliefs, 103–4, 170, 173, 175; body ornaments, 38, 100, 102–3; conquest of, 64–70, *71*, 73–9, 197; descent, 10, 97, 162–3, 197; domesticated animals, 152, 158; dress, 65, 105; dwellings, 20–1, *54*, 75, 98–103, 201–3; early post-conquest life, 79–85; fishing, 177–8; fortresses, *36*, 80, 83–5, 105–6, 109, 170; goat-horn uses, 66, 173, 177; Jandía wall, 55–6, 104–5; kingdoms, 105, 187; language, 29–30, 57, 152, 158, 168; medicine, 175; modern attitude towards, 182; name's origin, 105; navigation, 51–2; physical types, 96–7, 162–3; pottery, *54*, 99, 161–3; prehistory, 40–52, 55–63; privacy, 182; querns, 151; religious sanctuary, 103–4, 170, 201–3; round-ups, 158, 201–3; shellfish collecting, 100, 102, 177; slavery of, 16, 76, 79–85; spinning and weaving, 60; stature, 48–9; stone tools, 100, 208; storage cairns, 151; summer migration, 177; travertine pot-lids, 51, 99–100; vaulting staffs, 157–8; weapons, 109; *see also* Canary islanders, pre-conquest
Majadilla, 156
Majorata, 105
Majoreros, 105, 182
Majuelo, 161
Mallorcans, 64–6
Malocello, Lancelotto, 64
Malpaís, see Badlands
Man-hunts in Africa, 86–8, 92, 95–6
Manor houses, 110–12
Map, Spanish military, 10, 12
Marine fauna, 38–9
Marketing, co–operatives, 153–4,

INDEX